Psychology As Religion
The Cult of Self-Worship

by
Paul C. Vitz

William B. Eerdmans Publishing Company

Copyright © 1977 by William B. Eerdmans Publishing Co.
255 Jefferson Ave. S.E., Grand Rapids, Mich. 49503
All rights reserved
Printed in the United States of America

Third printing, February 1979

Library of Congress Cataloging in Publication Data

Vitz, Paul C   1935-
   Psychology as religion.

   Includes bibliographical references.
     1.   Psychology and religion.   2.   Psychology —
Philosophy.   3.   Self.   I.   Title.
BF51.V57   158   77-3403
ISBN 0-8028-1696-7

The author would like to thank the following publishers for permission to quote material from the books cited:

Harper and Row Publishing Company. *Motivation and Personality,* 2nd edition by Abraham Maslow. Copyright 1970.

Harper and Row Publishing Company. *The Phenomenon of Life* by Hans Jonas. Copyright 1966.

Harper and Row Publishing Company. *I'm OK — You're OK* by Thomas A. Harris, M.D. Copyright 1967, 1968, 1969 by Thomas A. Harris, M.D.

Harper and Row Publishing Company. *Carl Rogers on Encounter Groups* by Carl R. Rogers. Copyright 1973.

Harper and Row Publishing Company. *The Gulag Archipelago, III-IV* by Aleksandr Solzhenitsyn. Copyright 1975.

Basic Books, Inc. *The Discovery of the Unconscious: The History and Evolution of Dynamic Psychiatry* by Henri F. Ellenberger. Copyright 1970 by Henri F. Ellenberger. Basic Books, Inc.

Basic Books, Inc. *Existence: A New Dimension in Psychiatry and Psychology.* Rollo May, Ernest Angel, Henri F. Ellenberger (Editors). Copyright 1958. Basic Books, Inc.

For Timmie

Contents

Acknowledgments

This critique began as an informal paper presented in September 1974 to a small meeting of Episcopal clergy and laymen concerned with contemporary theological problems. The original talk grew into the present book primarily because many people along the way provided a great deal of the encouragement and support needed to get me to venture into the troubled waters of religion and popular psychology.

I am especially grateful for the frequent helpful criticisms given by Fathers Joseph Frary and J. Douglas Ousley; equal thanks are due to Professors Richard Mouw and Wayne Joosse, both of Calvin College, for their encouraging comments and analysis.

I have also been very much guided in the past few years by Father John Andrew, Rector of St. Thomas Church in New York — often, I am sure, without his knowing it. His moving, intelligent presentation of Christian spiritual life and doctrine, unadulterated with anti-Christian psychology, consistently reinforced the motivation behind this book.

As the reader may imagine, for someone who is a psychologist in a large and outstanding university department writing an extensive criticism of psychology is not without hazards. Yet many of my friends and colleagues in the psychology department at New York University have been generous in providing not only their time and criticisms but also their encouragement. They certainly do not agree with everything in the book, but their fairness and, above all, the constructive tone of their reactions have meant a great deal to me. In particular I would like to thank Professors Samuel Feldman, Karl Schick, Robert N. Sollod, and David Wolitzky. My admiration for them grows even in disagreement.

Others who at various times have given help which has been greatly appreciated are: Helen Corbett, Lewis Smedes, Canon William A. Johnson, Fr. Norman J. Catir, Jr., Fr. Livingston T. Merchant, Jr., and the Sisters at The House of the Redeemer.

Without doubt the strongest, steadiest help has come from my wife Timmie. Her thoughtful comments and her patience formed an environment in which the whole thing became possible.

—P.C.V.

About This Book

This book is for the reader interested in a critique of modern psychology — the reader who knows, perhaps only intuitively, that psychology has become more a sentiment than a science and is now part of the problem of modern life rather than part of its resolution. The varied criticisms offered here are scientific, philosophical, economic, ethical, and, finally, religious; their purpose is to provide arguments and concepts which allow the reader to begin the process of placing today's psychology in a much smaller, less corrosive, but ultimately more accurate and more helpful perspective than that which presently prevails.

As the title suggests, it will be argued that psychology has become a religion, in particular, a form of secular humanism based on worship of the self. A good deal of what follows by way of criticism, however, does not presuppose a religious orientation; and devotees of humanistic psychology (for example, of such concepts as self-actualization) are challenged to confront a psychologist's criticism of their widely accepted wisdom.

The major critical orientation of this book is Christian. This will be made most explicit in Chapters 6-8. Christianity, like all traditional religions, has a great deal at stake in this discussion. It may be noted that in those cases in which critical arguments are based on Christian doctrine, my conclusion is usually identical with or close to that which could be made by other religions. The present work is offered in a spirit of cooperation with other faiths, particularly

Judaism, in the common struggle against the influence of today's psychology.

Specifically, I shall argue for five theses:

1. Psychology as religion exists, and it exists in great strength throughout the United States.

2. Psychology as religion can be criticized on many grounds quite independent of religion.

3. Psychology as religion is deeply anti-Christian. Indeed, it is hostile to most religions.

4. Psychology as religion is extensively supported by schools, universities, and social programs financed by taxes collected from millions of Christians. This use of tax money to support what has become a secular state religion raises grave political and legal issues.

5. Psychology as religion has for years been destroying individuals, families, and communities. But for the first time the destructive logic of this secular religion is beginning to be understood, and as more and more people discover the emptiness of self-worship Christianity is presented with a major historical opportunity to provide meaning and life.

I make no apology for the intensity of some of my criticisms. The issues involved may be little acknowledged as yet, but they are very serious. The time has come for Christian academics and intellectuals to speak out publicly in defense of the faith regardless of the professional risk and isolation this may entail. Many of us are in strategic positions to observe and analyze anti-Christian trends in society which escape the notice of the theologians, who are often so busy fighting secularism in the seminaries that they have little time to keep up with other fields. Besides, many people would discount the arguments of theologians and clergy as nothing more than self-interested rationalizations of a dying institution.

* * *

Here a few autobiographical words are in order. Much of the subsequent analysis comes directly out of my personal experience as a student and as an academic psychologist during the last twenty years. I was an undergraduate at the University of Michigan from 1953 to 1957, a psychology major for the last three years. At college I followed a familiar script by rebelling against my nominally Christian upbringing. (This probably happens in high school now.) I read Bertrand Russell, announced I was an atheist, and took considerable pride in my hard-won independence. The only disappointment was that my announcement of it was met by others with what can best be described as a yawn.

My vague, superficial Christianity had been such weak stuff that its rejection had less psychological importance than, say, breaking up with my girl friend. In consequence, my period of active hostility to Christianity was quite brief: a few months in my sophomore year. After this began a long agnostic indifference to religion. It was a time I devoted fully to becoming a psychologist by concentrating on my graduate studies at Stanford University (1957-62). Here I majored in the subjects of motivation and personality, which included learning and teaching the views of the self-theorists.

In graduate school religion was treated as a pathetic anachronism. Occasionally a person's religious beliefs were "measured" in personality tests. The common interpretation was that people holding traditional religious views were fascist-authoritarian types. There was also some interest in religion on the part of social psychologists who wanted to study exotic belief systems. My contacts with the disciplines of anthropology and sociology suggested that similar attitudes were typical of people in these fields.

A year or so after I received my doctorate, my interests began to shift to experimental psychology, particularly the topics of perception, cognition, and aesthetics. This shift of interest was partly occasioned by a growing awareness that I found much humanistic personality theory false and rather silly. Many of the arguments presented here first occurred to me in the mid-1960s. I still remember moments in the middle of class lectures when I suddenly became aware that I was saying things I didn't believe. To discover you are teaching as a reasonable approximation to scientific truth something which you no longer think is true is disconcerting, to put it mildly.

This critical suspicion continued to grow. By 1968 or so I would no longer teach graduate or undergraduate courses that required me to cover the self-theorists. There things might have remained except for two unexpected events. One was the development of a nationwide mass enthusiasm for the humanistic self-theories about the same time that I was moving away from them. The other was my conversion to Christianity. There is nothing dramatic to report about the latter — no sudden rebirth or other mystical experience — just a great deal of intense emotional turbulence associated with the collapse of my secular ideals accompanied by a quietly growing change of heart and mind. This process seems to have started sometime in 1972, and at some point since then I discovered I was a Christian — a very poor one to be sure, but still my life has been turned around. The noteworthy aspect about this is that it happened to a totally unprepared, recalcitrant, secularized psychologist who thought that the only natural direction of change was exactly in the opposite direction. There were certainly no available models for it in psychology. Becoming a Christian provided me a dramatically different view of psychology as well as a strong motivation for developing some of the critical analysis I had begun several years earlier.

It is difficult to document such a thing as the general attitude of a profession. But the hostility of most psychologists to Christianity is very real. For years I was part of that sentiment; today it still surrounds me. It is a curious hostility, for most psychologists are not aware of it. Their lack of awareness is due mostly to sheer ignorance of what Christianity is — for that matter, of what any religion is. The universities are so secularized that most academics can no longer articulate why they are opposed to Christianity. They merely assume that for all rational people the question of being a Christian was settled — negatively — at some time in the past.

* * *

Finally, it is necessary to identify certain psychologies which will be explicitly excluded from our discussion. Experimental psychology — the study of sensation, perception, cognition, motivation, memory, problem solving, and related questions — is not included. This kind of psychology, primarily found in universities and research centers, is a branch of natural science composed of various amounts of biology, physics, mathematics, and so forth. Second, the theory or philosophy of psychology known as behaviorism (the best-known example is probably that of B. F. Skinner) is not treated here, since it has little in common with humanistic self-psychology, and criticism of it would carry our discussion quite far afield. There already has been much recent criticism of behaviorism, to which I have little to add.[1] Similarly, the therapeutic offspring of behaviorism known as behavior modification is excluded, since its techniques and principles are part of experimental psychology and its philosophy part of behaviorism.

A third omission is psychoanalysis, since much of self-psychology is a reaction against the more complex, "pessimistic," conservative, and disciplined Freudian theories and methods. To criticize psychoanalysis with any thoroughness would require technical discussion of much material that is unrelated to the self. This would lengthen the present discussion greatly and blur its major focus.*

I have not treated the interesting new development called transpersonal psychology.[2] This field (which might be better named "spiritual psychology" or perhaps "the psychology of

---

*Except in France where Freud's concepts are still having important effects, the influence of psychoanalysis is declining. In the United States it has been under consistent criticism from almost all quarters for a number of years. Certainly, many of the criticisms are overdue; yet, when the dust settles Freud's fundamental contributions will remain while today's minor theorists will soon be forgotten. During this period, when psychoanalysis is out of fashion, it may be a good time for Christianity quietly to work out an intellectual rapprochement between its own spiritual psychology and genuine psychoanalytic insights.

transcendent experience") is still too new for its character to be completely obvious. A critique of it would involve a direct comparative analysis of major religions as they are expressed in mystical or other transcendent activity. In any case, most of those participating in its development make no claim to be part of traditional Western psychological science (nor are their activities commonly funded through tax receipts).

One final group is excluded, namely, those psychologists who recognize, respect, and respond to genuine religious issues in the lives of their patients. This group is not large nor easily categorized. It includes psychologists who are personally committed to a religion, who integrate their faith, when appropriate, into therapy. But it also includes secular psychologists whose insights lead them to reject the contemporary religion of psychology as a superficial substitute for something genuine and a corruption of the important but limited function of psychotherapy. It is these psychologists who provide a basis for the hope that a strong, honest partnership may eventually develop between psychology and religion.

In spite of these exclusions, a large amount of modern psychology remains. In fact, most psychologists practicing today have been strongly affected by humanistic self-theories. Many American psychoanalysts have accepted so much of self-psychology that it is difficult to identify them as Freudian at all. Likewise, behavior modification therapists frequently espouse various self-actualizing philosophies in their own lives and as part of their professional ethic. Large numbers of transpersonal psychologists are still deeply rooted in self-theory and are just beginning to discover the serious conflict between the old self and the new transcendence. In short, America's eclectic tradition has meant that almost every form of psychology today comes with a large dose of the theories criticized here.

Psychology As Religion

Chapter One

Four Major Theorists

In the first two chapters I shall begin documenting the strong religious nature of much of today's psychology. In chapter one are presented in brief form the relevant theoretical positions of the four most important self-theorists — Erich Fromm, Carl Rogers, Abraham Maslow, and Rollo May. The popularizations of these and other self-theorists will be described briefly in the second chapter, with evidence of the widespread enthusiasm for their ideas. After this descriptive and summary material, criticisms of the self-theory position will be taken up in later chapters.

I have selected Fromm, Rogers, Maslow, and May as the "purest" and most influential self-theorists. Other psychologists have contributed to self-theory, but in general they have not been as completely committed to the concept of the self. The psychoanalytic ego-psychologists, for example, with their notions of the conflict-free ego sphere and ego mechanisms of defense, which were developed in the 1930s and 1940s by Heinz Hartmann and Anna Freud, are not pure self-psychologists, since they remained committed to much of traditional Freudian theory.[1] Emphasis on the self is also less extreme in the works of the famous earlier deviants from orthodox Freudianism — Jung, Rank, Adler, Horney. The recent work of R. D. Laing bears most directly on the nature of psychosis, rather than the more "normal" neurotic; apparently, he has been less influential, since he is rarely mentioned by the other self-theorists, though this may be because his work has not come into prominence until more recently.[2] Nevertheless, to the extent that these theorists whom we have omitted do emphasize the self, e.g. Adler, their ideas and impact are similar to the four we shall present below.

Erich Fromm

Erich Fromm was born in 1900, educated at Heidelberg, Frankfurt, and Munich, received psychoanalytic training in Berlin, and came to the United States in 1933. He has lived in the U.S. and Mexico most of the time since then. Fromm was originally a Freudian psychoanalyst, but he broke from this tradition in the 1930s. Fromm rejected Freud's emphasis on the biological nature of man, especially disputing Freud's inclusion of aggression (the death instinct) as a basic part of human nature. Freud gave aggression the same importance as sex (the life instinct), while in contrast Fromm emphasized society as the major determinant of human personality. In particular, Fromm describes man as intrinsically and naturally good and attributes anything bad — evil — to society, especially when society causes the self to deny its own potential for growth and expression. Except for the unconscious influence of society, Fromm has come to neglect the traditional psychoanalytic theory of the unconscious, for instance, dreams.

In spite of his break with the Freudian tradition, Fromm remains deeply influenced by Freud, often citing or criticizing him. He shares Freud's penchant for characterizing cultural belief systems and those who believe them in terms of psychological types, such as the "exploitative" and "marketing" character types of capitalist society or the "authoritative" and "regressive" beliefs characterizing the Christian doctrine of the Trinity.[3] The following remarks are typical of Fromm:

> A spirit of pride and optimism has distinguished Western culture in the last few centuries. . . . Man's pride has been justified. By virtue of his reason he has built a material world the reality of which surpasses even the dreams and visions of fairy tales and utopias. He harnesses physical energies which will enable the human race to secure the material conditions necessary for a dignified and productive

existence, and although many of his goals have not yet been attained there is hardly any doubt they are within reach and that *the problem of production* — which was the problem in the past — is, in principle, solved.[4]

Elsewhere in the same book he speaks in the same optimistic vein of human character:

> I shall attempt to show that the character structure of the mature and integrated personality, the productive character, constitutes the source and basis of "virtue," and that "vice," in the last analysis, is indifference to one's own self and self-mutilation. Not self-renunciation nor selfishness but the affirmation of his truly human self, are the supreme values of humanistic ethics. If man is to have confidence in values, he must know himself and the capacity of his nature for goodness and productiveness.[5]

In this view, a value such as love for one's neighbor is not viewed as a phenomenon *transcending* man;

> it is something inherent and *radiating from* him. Love is not a higher power which descends upon man nor a duty which is imposed upon him; it is his own power by which he relates himself to the world and makes it truly his.[6]

This of course has consequences for one's idea of what human nature is in itself:

> The position taken by humanistic ethics that man is able to know what is good and to act accordingly on the strength of his natural potentialities and of his reason, would be untenable if the dogma of man's innate natural evilness were true.[7]

Fromm's hostility to Christianity is clear in *The Dogma of Christ*, where he argues that belief in God *always* functions as "the ally of the rulers" (a position he must find difficult to reconcile with the persecution of Christian believers by atheistic rulers in, say, the Soviet Union, Albania, or China). Fromm claims that Christianity arose from a proletariat class so frustrated in its hopes for political and social change that it turned to salvation in a fantasy world of the supernatural.[8] His own religious position is quite explicit in *You Shall Be*

As Gods: the concept of God has evolved to the point that man is God; and, if the sacred exists, its center is in the self and the selves of others. Fromm's ideal society is humanistic, communitarian socialism, which he presents in considerable detail in *The Sane Society* (1955).

Throughout Fromm's works his atheism and materialism, his political views and other values so permeate his psychology that it is hard to sort out those contributions which might reasonably be considered scientific.

Carl Rogers

Carl Rogers, a midwestern American, was born in 1902. He describes himself as "the middle child in a large, close-knit family where hard work and a highly conservative Protestant Christianity were about equally revered."[9] He was graduated in 1924 from the University of Wisconsin, having switched from agricultural science to preparation for the ministry. He attended Union Theological Seminary in New York City, where he was exposed to a liberal philosophical viewpoint regarding religion. After a short visit abroad he broke from Christianity, deciding that he wanted to help humanity without being inhibited by any prior commitment to a fixed set of beliefs whose truth was not obvious to him. He transferred to the Teachers College at Columbia, where he was influenced by John Dewey's thought, and received the Ph.D. degree in 1928.

From Rogers' varied exposure to different psychological theories he developed his own position which has become highly influential. For the present we shall omit discussion of his technique of therapy called "non-directive," or "client-centered," and concentrate on his theory of personality and the goals of therapy. The central work for our purposes is *On Becoming a Person.* Here Rogers states the goal of therapy as follows:

> If I can create a relationship characterized on my part: by a genuiness and transparency, *in which I am my real feelings; by a warm acceptance of and prizing of the other person as a separate individual;* by a sensitive ability to see his world and himself

as he sees them; then the other individual in the relationship: will experience and understand aspects of himself which previously he has repressed; will find *himself becoming better integrated,* more able to function effectively; will become more similar to the person he would like to be; will be *more self-directing and self-confident;* will become *more of a person, more unique and more self-expressive;* will be more understanding, more acceptant of others; will be able to cope with the problems of life more adequately and more comfortably. I believe this statement holds whether I am speaking of my relationship with a client, with a group of students or staff members, with my family or children. It seems to me that *we have here a general hypothesis which offers exciting possibilities for the development of creative, adaptive, autonomous persons.* [10]

Psychotherapy, once a restricted and specialized activity, is now generalized to all of life's relations. Exactly how far this goes will be noted later. Rogers' writings are much more oriented toward the process of therapy than Fromm's, and he tends to ignore large cultural and historical themes. He interprets therapy as a process of the changing and growing self:

Throughout the discussion which follows, I shall assume that the *client experiences himself as being fully received.* By this I mean that whatever his feelings — fear, despair, insecurity, anger; whatever his mode of expression — silence, gestures, tears, or words; whatever he finds himself being in this moment, *he senses that he is psychologically received, just as he is, by the therapist.* [11]

The presumptive religious quality is apparent.

More explicitly, Rogers describes his theory of therapy as follows:

Individuals move, I began to see, not from a fixity or homeostasis through change to a new fixity, though such a process is indeed possible. But much the more significant continuum is from fixity to changingness, from rigid structure to flow, from stasis to process. I formed the tentative hypothesis that perhaps the qualities of the client's expression at any one point might indicate his position on this continuum, might indicate where he stood in the process of change. [12]

At the first stage (of seven) the person is fixed, static, completely blocked; he is either unaware of his feelings and emotions or attributes them to objective external circumstances. By Stage 2 or 3 we have people described as follows:

> Example: "And yet there is the matter of, well, how much do you leave yourself open to marriage, and if your professional vocation is important, and that's the one thing that's really yourself at this point, it does place a limitation on your contact."
>
> In this excerpt her self is such a remote object that this would probably best be classified as being between stages two and three.
>
> *There is also expression about the self as a reflected object, existing primarily in others.*
>
> *There is much expression about or description of feelings and personal meanings not now present.*
>
> *There is very little acceptance of feelings. For the most part feelings are revealed as something shameful, bad, or abnormal, or unacceptable in other ways.*[13]

The fifth stage Rogers describes this way:

> *Feelings are expressed freely as in the present.*
>
> Example: "I expect kinda to get a severe rejection — this I expect all the time . . . somehow I guess I even feel it with you. . . . It's hard to talk about because I want to be the best I can possibly be with you."
>
> *Feelings are very close to being fully experienced. They "bubble up," "seep through," in spite of the fear and distrust which the client feels at experiencing them with fullness and immediacy.*
>
> Example: "That kinda came out and I just don't understand it. (*Long pause*) I'm trying to get hold of what that terror is."
>
> Example: Client is talking about an external event. Suddenly she gets a pained, stricken look.
>
> Therapist: "What — what's hitting you now?"
>
> Client: "I don't know. (*She cries*) . . . I must have been getting a little too close to something I didn't want to talk about, or something."[14]

The culmination of Rogerian therapy is the seventh and highest stage, which is summarized as follows.

The process moves from a point of fixity, where all the
elements and threads described are separately discernible and
separately understandable, to the flowing peak moments of
therapy in which all these threads become inseparably woven
together. In the new experiencing with immediacy which
occurs at such moments, feeling and cognition interpenetrate,
self is subjectively present in the experience, volition is
simply the subjective following of a harmonious balance of
organismic direction. Thus, as the process reaches this point
the person becomes a unity of flow, or motion. He has changed,
but what seems most significant, he has become an integrated
process of changingness.[15]

Abraham Maslow

Like Rogers, Abraham Maslow, born in 1908, was educated
at the University of Wisconsin. He spent his early academic
years in New York City at Columbia Teachers College and
Brooklyn College. His independently developed theory of the
self is close to Rogers' but his distinctive concepts deserve
mention.

Maslow postulates a hierarchy of human needs. This
hierarchy, whose basis is assumed to be innate, requires
that needs must be satisfied in a relatively fixed order,
starting with basic physiological and safety needs, proceeding
to needs for belonging and love, for self-esteem and status,
and finally reaching the highest need, the need for self-
realization, or self-actualization as Maslow calls it. This
last need is the most distinctively human, although it depends
for fulfilment on the prior satisfaction of the lower needs.
The person in whom this final need is satisfied is the self-
actualized person, an ideal type whose distinctive characteristics are:

(1) efficient perceiving of reality and comfortableness
with it;

(2) acceptance of self and others;

(3) spontaneity;

(4) an autonomous self independent of culture;

(5) creativity (a universal hallmark of the ideal person
among self-theorists);

(6) having "peak" experiences, that is, oceanic or mystic experiences; and

(7) democratic, egalitarian, and humanitarian character structure and values.[16]

Maslow's description of the essential quality of these self-actualized types is revealing:

> A few centuries ago these would all have been described as men who walk in the path of God or as godly men. A few say that they believe in God, but describe this God more as a metaphysical concept than as a personal figure. If religion is defined only in social-behavioral terms, then these are all religious people, the atheist included. But if more conservatively we use the term religion so as to include and stress the supernatural element and institutional orthodoxy (certainly the more common usage) then our answer must be quite different, for then almost none of them is religious.
>
> [Creativeness] is a universal characteristic of all the people studied or observed. There is no exception. Each one shows in one way or another a special kind of creativeness or originality or inventiveness that has certain peculiar characteristics. . . . For one thing, it is different from the special creativeness of the Mozart type. We may as well face the fact that so-called geniuses display ability that we do not understand. All we can say of them is that they seem to be specially endowed with a drive and a capacity that may have rather little relationship to the rest of the personality and with which, from all evidence, the individuals seem to be born. Such talent we have no concern with here since it does not rest upon psychic health or basic satisfaction. The creativeness of the self-actualized man seems rather to be kin to the naive and universal creativeness of unspoiled children.[17]

Maslow names some of these secular saints — Lincoln in his last days, Thomas Jefferson, Einstein, Eleanor Roosevelt, Jane Addams, William James, Spinoza, and aspects of Walt Whitman, Thoreau, Beethoven, George Washington Carver, Goethe, Fritz Kreisler, Eugene V. Debs, Thomas Eakins, Albert Schweitzer, and so on.[18]

Rollo May

Our last theorist is Rollo May. Born in 1909, he received the Bachelor of Arts degree from Oberlin, a Bachelor of Divinity from Union Theological Seminary, and the Ph.D. at Columbia Teachers College. (Thus his educational background is remarkably similar to that of Rogers and Maslow: all moved from states in the Great Lakes area to New York City and Columbia Teachers College — and in two cases attended Union Seminary across the street.) May's special contribution to self-theory comes from the European influence of existentialism, which he first encountered in his psychotherapeutic studies in Vienna.

Existentialism as a philosophy is notoriously hard to characterize rigorously, and existential therapy has the same difficulty. It is, however, possible to isolate some special themes in existential therapy which represent a distinctive existential strand in the framework of self-theory.

The central concept is probably that of "being there" (*Dasein*), by which is meant the intense fundamental awareness of one's existence. This basic experience is described by a patient of May's, a young woman who reported:

> Then what is left? What is left is this, "I am." This act of contact and acceptance with "I am," once gotten hold of, gave me (what I think was for me the first time) the experience since I am, I have the right to be.
>
> What is this experience like? . . . It is the experience of my own aliveness not caring whether it turns out to be an ion or just a wave. . . . It is my saying to Descartes, "I AM, therefore, I think, I feel, I do." [19]

This "I am" experience is the basic experience of being, and although it is not itself a solution to a patient's problem, he claims that it is a necessary precondition for successful analysis.

One important property of being is that it rejects the distinction between the knowing or experiencing subject and the known or experienced object. Instead, the concept of being is a basic part of the existentialist "endeavor to understand man by cutting below the cleavage between subject and object which has bedeviled Western thought and science since shortly after the Renaissance." [20] This condition of being is inseparable from its opposite — the condition of non-being or nothingness. Awareness of and confrontation with non-being, especially in the form of death, gives rise to the powerful and pervasive emotion of *Angst* (dread or anxiety). Therefore, at the very center of existentialist thought is the common modern condition of pervasive anxiety which is "the experience of the threat of imminent non-being."[21]

This existence takes place in a world or universe characterized as Being-in-the-world. The three aspects of the existential world are the *Umwelt* (the "world around," the environment), the *Mitwelt* (the "world with" others, our life of social and interpersonal relations), and most central, the *Eigenwelt* (the "own world," the world of the self and relationship to one's self). Two or all three of these worlds may be experienced at the same time but taken together they are the *only* arenas within which our existence takes place.

An important existential concept is "becoming," the process of self-development or fulfilling one's potential. This process unfolds by way of the self's choosing its own course of self-fulfilment. Acts of choice bring the self from its initial existence into an actualized self, with a nature or essence created by its choice. Thus, the self first exists (i.e., "I am") but without any a priori nature or essence. Instead, through acts of choice the self's essence is created. These choices are courageously made in the face of the self's awareness of non-being and its experience of *Angst*. Guilt arises through failure to develop the self's potential, through blocking or ignoring one's chance to become one's potential. Transcendence is the name of the important capacity of the existential self to surpass or climb beyond the prior level of self-development. Thus, as self-potential is developed each new stage is a transcending of the earlier stages and this process often is called "becoming."

May points out that Carl Rogers, although he never had direct contact with existentialism, has developed a therapy with important existential aspects, especially in Rogers' emphases on becoming and on the therapist's direct experience of himself and of the patient.

> I launch myself into the therapeutic relationship having a hypothesis, or a faith, that my liking, my confidence, and my

understanding of the other person's inner world, will lead to a significant process of becoming. I enter the relationship not as a scientist, not as a physician who can accurately diagnose and cure, but as a person, entering into a personal relationship. Insofar as I see him only as an object, the client will tend to become only an object.[22]

A final significant point is the claim of existential psychology that a natural science of human beings is not possible. Jean-Paul Sartre expresses this as a refusal "to consider man as capable of being analyzed and reduced to original givens, to determined desires (or drives), supported by the subject as properties [are] by an object."[23]

In summary, existential therapy starts with the isolated self, aware of its basic existence but confronted by non-existence and the associated emotion of dread. This self, valued and accepted directly by the therapist, is encouraged, in the face of non-being, courageously to commit its self to self-defined decisions that will bring its potential to fulfilment. This transcendent activity, or becoming-through-choosing, also creates the essence of the individual. On the other hand, failure to fulfil self-potential causes guilt. When this process succeeds, an individual who initially had only an existence has now created his own essence.

This self-knowledge is arrived at by the patient's learning the meaning of his experienced states on their own terms, that is, phenomenologically and not via some "objective" subject-object philosophy, as found in natural science. All of this takes place in a universe limited to three aspects: the external environment, the social and interpersonal environment, and the self and its relation to itself.

Chapter Two

Self-Theory for Everybody

Fromm, Rogers, Maslow, and May are all theoreticians. No matter how influential their concepts have been with intellectuals and students, they had to be translated into popular form before they could reach large numbers of people. Some of those who have done this job of translating have pushed the ideas of these four theorists to extremes for which they should not be held responsible. Yet it should be borne in mind that the popularizers are primarily professional psychologists or psychiatrists, and their works do represent a legitimate presentation or logical extension of self-theory. Actually the line between "theorist" and "popularizer" cannot be drawn all that precisely. None of the four preceding theorists is likely to merit classification as a major thinker. At best they introduce interesting and useful but limited concepts. A good number of their recent works are indistinguishable from popularization: I am thinking especially of Rogers' *Carl Rogers on Encounter Groups* (1970) and *Becoming Partners: Marriage and Its Alternatives* (1972), which are discussed below.

Keep in mind that many of the particular expressions of self-theory, such as those we shall describe, are apt to be very short-lived. Despite their prominence a few years ago, encounter groups, for instance, seem to have all but disappeared. But new forms of popularized self-theory continually arise, and they all have apparently important effects on many of their participants.

Encounter Groups

The important and special environment for spreading self-theory has been the small group generally known as an encounter group. According to Rogers, these groups, which come in many varieties, among them T-groups, Gestalt therapy, and creativity workshops, have the following common characteristics:

> A facilitator can develop, in a group which meets intensively, a psychological climate of safety in which freedom of expression and reduction of defensiveness gradually occur.
>
> A climate of mutual trust develops out of this mutual freedom to express real feelings, positive and negative. Each member moves toward greater acceptance of his total being — emotional, intellectual and physical — as it *is*, including its potential.
>
> With individuals less inhibited by defensive rigidity, the possibility of change in personal attitudes and behavior, in professional methods, in administrative procedures and relationships, becomes less threatening.
>
> There is a development of feedback from one person to another, such that each individual learns how he appears to others and what impact he has in interpersonal relationships.
>
> With this greater freedom and improved communication, new ideas, new concepts, new directions emerge. Innovation can become a desirable rather than a threatening possibility.
>
> These learnings in the group experience tend to carry over, temporarily or more permanently, into the relationships with spouse, children, students, subordinates, peers, and even superiors following the group experience.[1]

I shall not go into examples of encounter group interactions, since this identification should be adequate for those who are not already familiar, at least in a general way, with what encounter groups are. Undoubtedly, the last decade has seen the formation of hundreds of thousands of such groups, actively involving millions of Americans. Rogers estimates that the number of encounter group participants in one year, 1970, was probably three quarters of a million.

Self-Helpers

The first important popularization of self-theory came in 1964 with the publication of Eric Berne's *Games People Play*, which was to sell over three million copies. Berne represents personality as made up only of ego states (non-ego aspects of personality are entirely ignored). These states are: (1) those which resemble parental figures; (2) those which are autonomously directed toward objective appraisal of reality; and (3) those which represent archaic relics — ego states fixated in early childhood which are still active. These states are usually called the Parent, Adult, and Child, respectively, with undesirable behavior being caused by the Parent and Child states. The popularity of Berne's book presumably reflects his ability to describe the transactions between people, or "games," with clarity and wit. His particular formulation of self-theory is known as *transactional analysis*. The goal of his therapy is to help people become autonomous adults characterized by spontaneity, unbiased awareness of reality, and candid intimacy with others.

Following from and developing Berne's theory was *I'm OK — You're OK* by Thomas Harris. Published in 1968, this book has sold over a million hardcover copies, and has gone through more than a dozen paperback printings. In this form of transactional analysis, too, the three ego states — Parent, Adult, and Child — are the three psychic actors, and again the goal is to develop creative and growing human relationships free from fear. Recent transactional analysts have focused specifically on business success and winning in the game of life — "You were born to win" is the motif.[2]

Two other popular books in the self-realization category are Nathaniel Branden's *Breaking Free* (1972) and *The Psychology of Self-Esteem* (1969). Branden's goal is to develop the personal autonomy and self-esteem essential to an individual's well-being. Similarly, Jess Lair in *I Ain't Much, Baby — But I'm All I've Got* (1969) proclaims that his book will help you "free yourself through this proven program of self-acceptance, self-enrichment and love." *Person to Person* (1967) by Carl Rogers and Barry Stevens would fit into this category, as would books presenting Frederick Perls'

Gestalt Therapy.[3] To provide any kind of complete catalog of the various popular self-theories is almost impossible, since the public appetite for this sort of book seems insatiable. Many bookstores now have psychological self-help sections, where one will find numerous other titles similar to those covered here.

An interesting recent variant of self-help is assertiveness training — therapy aimed at making the shy, timid, or withdrawn person more capable of assertion in interpersonal situations. In a typical session the client is put in a role-playing situation where he can make aggressive, independent responses to the therapist, who plays the role of someone attempting to take advantage of him. The result of these practice sessions is presumably an increase in the person's self-assertiveness. Not only does this training value assertiveness, but also frequently involves devaluing love. Some of the more forceful advocates of this training see compassion and assertiveness as psychologically contradictory and argue that a liberated woman, for example, should escape the "compassion traps" in which so many women are caught.

A best-selling application to the business world of the same philosophy of blatant self-aggrandizement has recently been published by Robert J. Ringer under the title *Winning Through Intimidation*. This handbook for personal success argues that winning in business and personal transactions depends on assuming an intimidating and assertive posture. Ringer claims to offer a realistic program for personal success. The injunction that we are to be concerned with our neighbor's good he dismisses as a ploy used by others against us.[4]

est

Although it is clearly a very popular form of self-theory, est (Erhard Seminar Training) introduces some significant new characteristics.[5] In the first place, est is primarily a business, efficiently directed by its founder and head Werner Erhard for the purpose of making a profit. Indeed, the internal discipline of the organization is so strong that its style of operation has been labeled fascist. Beginning in 1971, it has grown to a multi-million-dollar operation, involving a core of highly trained seminar leaders plus a staff of six thousand volunteers. Seminars are four-day marathon sessions with as many as 250 participants, who have paid $250 for the complete series. The seminars require a disciplined, well-trained leader and participants who are willing obediently to follow the rules throughout the sixty-hour experience. These marathon sessions have some similarities with old-style, lengthy revival meetings, but their setting, in fancy large hotels, is quite different.

Seminar leaders are trained to resemble as closely as possible both the teaching and personality of Werner Erhard. The main goal of the training is to get the participants to "transform their ability to *experience* living." The key word is *experience*, since the main thrust is not on new ways to believe or think but on new ways to experience. To this end various techniques are used, all of which are centered around the participants' self. The techniques come from a variety of sources — encounter groups, Maslow, Gestalt therapy, Zen, and Scientology. Although a few techniques borrowed from Eastern religion give est training a distinctively "spiritual" flavor — at least by comparison with earlier self-therapy — the overwhelming emphasis is still on the self.

Listen to some samples of its remarkable philosophy, quoted from the recent book *est: Playing the Game the New Way,* by Carl Frederick, an est graduate:[6]

> *You* are the Supreme being.
>
> Reality is a reflection of your notions. Totally. Perfectly.
>
> So you got the notion to play a little game with yourself. That is, you said to yourself, something like, "Gee, this is rather boring. Wouldn't it be more FUN to COMMUNICATE." So you created a WORD game. That's all life is — one big word game. Don't lie to yourself about it anymore. They even wrote it down, not long after the beginning. They said: "AND THE WORD WAS GOD."
>
> Of course it was.
>
> Also notice that there isn't any right/wrong — it simply doesn't make SENSE to be unethical.

> You had the notion that communicating would be more fun. And you created all the rules. So you are responsible for the game as it is. All of it.
>
> And it has no significance. You're IT. Choose. It has no significance. Choose. Life is one big, "SO WHAT?" "CHOOSE."

This particular book ends with a pure Rogerian position mixed with a popularized existentialist concern with choice.

> And human beings who LET GO and simply experience life that way, as I observe things, usually end up being happy, loving, self-expressive and healthy.
>
> . . . Letting go of the notions they told you about, and creating your own.
>
> That's what aliveness is all about.
>
> You see, in my view, the sole purpose of life is to acknowledge that you're the source, then choose to BE what you know you are. It'll all flow from there.

If you think Frederick has trivialized and distorted the original message in his popularization, a comparison of his views with that of Carl Rogers will be revealing. For example, Rogers says explicitly: "I am the one who chooses" and "I am the one who determines the value of an experience for me."[7] Even more interesting is a comparison of Frederick with the weighty existential philosophy of Jean-Paul Sartre:

> If I've discarded God the father, there has to be someone to invent values. . . . To say that we invent values means nothing else but this: life has no meaning *a priori*. Before you come alive, life is nothing; it's up to you to give it a meaning, and value is nothing else but the meaning that you choose.[8]

So far, over sixty thousand people, typically professionals and other well-educated upper-middle-class participants, have paid to hear this amazingly literal self-deification combined with a belief in the ability of the omnipotent self to choose happiness and health and thus win at the game of life. All this is done in spite of the belief that the game of life has no intrinsic significance or meaning.

Self-Help Sex

Although we have not mentioned it in our discussion to this point, one of the major ways of being receptive to experience and expressing love is through sex. All of the authors we have discussed advocate openness to sex and active discovery and exploration of sex. Such enormously popular manuals as Alex Comfort's *Joy of Sex* (1972) and *More Joy* (1974) owe much of their success to people influenced by self-theory. John Money, advancing a position similar to Comfort's, advocates what he calls the new "recreational" sex, in contrast to the old "procreational" sex, no longer seen as functional.[9]

The connection between the "Money and Comfort" recreational theory of sex and self-theory comes in part from the importance given by the latter to avoiding culturally determined inhibitions and to being open, especially to interpersonal and sensual experience. Then, too, sex is easily interpreted as an expression of love. Taken together these factors have made sex a primary emphasis of self-theory. The essential guiding principle can be stated as sex in the service of the ego.

In the best-seller *Open Marriage* authors Nena and George O'Neill argue that sexual fidelity should be redefined, so as to eliminate the elements of duty and obligation, which they see as threats to love, growth, and trust.

> Fidelity . . . is redefined in open marriage, as commitment to your own growth, equal commitment to your partner's growth, and a sharing of the self-discovery accomplished through such growth. It is loyalty and faithfulness to growth, to integrity and to self and respect for the other, not to a sexual and psychological bondage to each other.
>
> In an open marriage, in which each partner is secure in his own identity and trusts in the other, new possibilities for additional relationships exist, and open (as opposed to limited) love can expand to include others. . . .
>
> These outside relationships may, of course, include sex. That is completely up to the partners involved. If partners in an open marriage do have outside sexual relationships, it is on the basis of their own internal relationships — that

is, because they have experienced mature love, have real trust, and are able to expand themselves, to love and enjoy others and to bring that love and pleasure back into their marriage, without jealousy.[10]

The degree to which the argument for open sex in marriage quite naturally goes is illustrated by Caroline Gordon's *Beginner's Guide to Group Sex*. This book takes the O'Neills' thesis and argues aggressively that exchanging marriage partners for sex, euphemistically called "swinging," is a true sign of a good, mature marriage. After all, a self-fulfilled, non-jealous man and woman should be experience-seeking, relaxed about something so natural as sex. Gordon describes the technique and manners of group sex in sections with titles like: "What to Wear at an Orgy," "Who Does What to Whom and How," "Stimulants and Implements," and "Pardon Me While I Get My Boots and Whip." In sum, group sex is seen simply as a question of pleasure. The conclusion reveals just how casual these decisions are considered to be:

> Just as one shoe size does not fit everyone, neither does one cohabitation contract — or marriage contract — fit everyone either. It is best to explore and to discover what feels most "comfortable" to you and your mate. After all, the choice between Swinging and not Swinging is not irrevocable, anymore than sampling frog's legs is. If you find you like frog's legs, continue to order them, if you don't, you never have to try them again. Like frog's legs, Swinging can be continued, dropped, or practiced in moderation or abundance once tried. Each couple has the freedom to decide what best fits their taste.[11]

Despite the sale of millions of copies of the many guidebooks to marital and sexual satisfaction which are available, the number of divorces continues to climb. The recent increases in the rate of marital dissolution owe much to the values advanced by self-theory, at least if the comments of former partners can be taken at face value. Especially explosive is the combination of the values of self-theory with a strident version of feminism. Not surprisingly, women are insisting that they have the right to lead the same self-preoccupied kind of life many men have been living for years. Perhaps it should be apparent that a high degree of assertive autonomy is impossible in any serious long-term human relationship, much less one involving the duties of genuine love and the sacrifices of parenthood, but as we have seen such notions as duty and sacrifice are rejected by today's popular self-theory counselors and therapists. We shall return to this subject later, particularly in Chapter 7.

Chapter Three

Selfism As Bad Science

From the description of the preceding chapter it is no doubt becoming clear that self-theory is a widely popular, secular, and humanistic ideology or "religion," not a branch of science. We shall offer further evidence of the religious character of self-theory later, but for our present purpose of showing that self-psychology commonly *functions* as a religion it is appropriate to use Fromm's definition of religion: "any system of thought and action shared by a group which gives the individual a frame of orientation and an object of devotion."[1] To place this in context let us cite a very important example of the religious claims of humanism from John Dewey. Dewey concludes his book *A Common Faith* with an exhortation to make humanism an active "common faith": in humanism "are all the elements of a religious faith that shall not be confined to sect, class, or race. Such a faith has always been implicitly the common faith of mankind. *It remains to make it explicit and militant.*"[2]

Fromm's definition and Dewey's exhortation set in bold relief the aggressive ideological character of the kind of secular humanism we have been talking about, with its devotion to the "self" and to "man." We shall use the term "selfism" to refer to this religion and its rationale for self-expression, creativity, and the like. We shall avoid terms like "selfishness" and "egotism," which do not accurately describe the modern phenomenon and have in any event lost much of their critical sting.

Before taking up specific criticisms in the next chapters,

let us note a very general one. Selfist psychology emphasizes the human capacity for change to the point of almost totally ignoring the idea that life has limits and that knowledge of them is the basis of wisdom. For selfists there seem to be no acceptable duties, denials, inhibitions, or restraints. Instead, there are only rights and opportunities for change. An overwhelming number of the selfists assume that there are no unvarying moral or interpersonal relationships, no permanent aspects to individuals. All is written in sand by a self in flux.[3] The tendency to give a green light to any self-defined goal is undoubtedly one of the major appeals of selfism, particularly to young people in a culture in which change has long been seen as intrinsically good.

Psychiatry, Biology, and Experimental Psychology

The scientific criticism of selfism comes from three major sources: (1) psychoanalysis and psychiatry; (2) studies on animal behavior, such as those by biologists or ethologists; and (3) the research of experimental psychologists. All three disciplines make the same point: that aggression, including destructive aggression, is a natural, intrinsic property of humans, present from birth.

Psychiatrists of many persuasions reject selfism as a throwback to the rationalistic, optimistic, superficial, and completely conscious interpretation of mind common in the eighteenth and nineteenth centuries. One of Freud's widely acknowledged achievements was to conceptualize the powerful unconscious, irrational elements in human nature. Many have rejected his scheme of binary opposition between the life instincts (e.g., sex) and the death instincts (e.g., aggression). But the clinical evidence, assembled over many years from a large and heterogeneous group of people, for such behaviors as sadism, destructiveness, and repetitive and terrifying dreams is considered overwhelming. Instead of convoluted optimistic explanations about how society causes such things it is simpler and more economical from a theoretical point of view to accept the intrinsic dual nature of man.

From the perspective of "depth" psychologists and others

who work with the seriously disturbed, selfism is a superficial theory causing occasional short-term positive effects in people who are already healthy or in those with only trivial neurotic difficulties. The position of Jacques Lacan, a prominent French psychoanalyst, is summarized by Jeffrey Mehlman:

> Lacan's break with American ego psychology, which he has denounced as the ideology of free enterprise, is thorough. Whereas the American theorists have retained the Freudian notion of the ego as an agent of synthesis, mastery, integration, and adaptation, Lacan's point of departure . . . has been to revive a far more worrisome conception of the ego, which is implicit in Freud's papers on narcissism and on mourning and melancholia. . . . The Americans write of ego mastery, Lacan's ruse has been to situate that mastery in a (Hegelian) dialect of master and slave. What for the Americans is an agent of strength, for Lacan is the victim of the illusion of strength; the would be guardian of objectivity is the ideologue *par excellence,* whose main function is to insulate the ego from the scandal of primary process thinking.[4]

Ethologists — for example, Nobel laureates Konrad Lorenz and Niko Tinbergen — fully accept aggression as one of the basic characteristics of animals, especially the primates and man in particular. They see aggression as usually quite functional in maintaining social organization and in keeping other groups of the same species at a reasonable distance. Warding off predators also has obvious benefits. To an ethologist, aggression, like all traits, can be either "good," that is, functional, or "bad," that is, dysfunctional, depending on the circumstance in which it is being displayed. As for the claim that man is naturally without aggression, that is preposterous. Indeed, our very success and dominance as a species strongly suggests we have too much of it. Both Lorenz and Tinbergen believe that man's aggressive capacity is now out of balance with recent cultural changes and they carry on a lively debate over the exact nature of our aggression and how to control it.[5] Even biologist René Dubos, a prominent humanist, who shares many values with the self-theorists, nevertheless assumes that any analysis of human potential must start with aggression as a basic property of our character. He writes, "In view of the fact that human beings evolved as hunters, it is not surprising that they have inherited a biological propensity to kill."[6]

Ludwig von Bertalanffy is another prominent biologist and humanist who accepts the potential for good and evil as intrinsic to human nature. He argues on purely biological grounds that basic moral codes, such as those forbidding murder, rape, stealing, and the like, are needed for survival. Even strong positive bonds of comradeship and love are biologically needed. He notes that behavior consistent with such ethical standards is common to many social animals and primitive human groups. For Bertalanffy basic ethics thus consists simply of verbalized instincts. He goes on to develop an interesting interpretation of the basis of human violence by arguing that the essential human characteristic is the ability to symbolize. And it is the "clash between ideologies or symbols," not the need for biological survival, which is the origin of war. In other words, war is the natural outcome of human aggressiveness expressed in the most distinctive human form — our symbol systems. The Old Testament story of the origin of evil he finds remarkably accurate. He paraphrases it in this way: "Thus man has to pay for the uniqueness that distinguishes him from other beings. The tree of knowledge is the tree of death."[7]

That the expression of so-called positive drives like sex can be dysfunctional is rarely considered by the popularizers of selfism — and indeed scarcely more often by the major theorists. For example, even sado-masochism is receiving good press lately from books like *Joy of Sex, More Joy,* and *Group Sex.* Recently an entire book has appeared defending the thesis that sado-masochism is fine if you like it, and if you haven't tried it don't criticize it.[8] That in satisfying our biological hungers we often devour ourselves and others receives little or no emphasis from self-theorists, despite the well-documented psychological principle that the adaptation level for pleasure (or the level for optimum stimulation by our environment) constantly moves up with experience. This "relativity of pleasure" pushes people to more and more extreme situations just to keep the amount of pleasure constant. In practice, this leads to diminishing pleasure, because of the increasingly negative side-effects of the more extreme conditions.[9] The psychologist Donald Campbell has noted in marriage and other personal relationships the common contemporary phenomenon of rising expectations of pleasure combined with a rising adaptation level which can result in frustration ,of the sort which destroys so many present-day marriages. He suggests that a doctrine emphasizing duty instead of one promising pleasure might produce an overall higher amount of satisfaction.[10]

Maslow has cited various types of evidence in support of his assumption that human nature contains only potential for good. Cofer and Appley, in their well-known text *Motivation: Research and Theory,* argue that this limited scientific evidence — for example, the unconscious regulation (or homeostasis) of certain body functions, self-selection of diet in children and animals — is only distantly relevant and quite weak. They write further:

> Another evidence for his view of human nature, suggested by Maslow, is that children are natural, spontaneous, undefensive, curious and, in their way, creative to an extent greater than the typical adult or older child in our culture. This is a point with which it is difficult to disagree, although we can find few satisfactory data that would directly validate it in other than an impressionistic way. Again, of course, it is difficult to say why such characteristics are taken as supporting a universal view of human nature without also mentioning that children are often irritable, impulsive, short-sighted, aggressive, egocentric and bound by physiological needs.[11]

As for Maslow's well-known concept of "self-actualization" the few data which have been published are ambiguous, and far too meager to support the large importance attached to the concept. For unknown reasons Maslow, in investigating his self-actualized subjects, did not take the elementary precaution of having a control group! As a result, we know little of how the self-actualized people were selected for this sample and studied. We know nothing about their social and economic status or their early childhood. Their marriages, family life, number of children, or geographical and religious background are not described to any useful degree of specificity.[12] It seems likely that they were especially intelligent, educated, talented, and physically healthy. Nearly any of these uncontrolled factors could make the sample atypical and thus highly unsuitable as a population from which to generalize about the motivational potential of the entire human race.

Carl Rogers initiated some of the first very primitive empirical studies of psychotherapy by tape recording therapy interviews and analyzing the recordings, usually in a qualitative manner. He was also instrumental in some early investigations of the patients' self-concepts using a technique developed by Stephenson called the Q-sort.[13] But despite the promise of these initial attempts, subsequent research by Rogers and his followers has been minimal. In fact, his emphasis has shifted so much in the opposite direction that he now attacks psychology as having a one-sided and arbitrary focus on methodology and research design.[14] In response, prominent clinical psychologists like Hans Strupp have charged that Rogers and his followers are a major source of fuzzy-minded irrationalism and a serious threat to the scientific integrity of clinical psychology.[15]

When pressed, self-theorists argue that their ideas are in fact based on extensive empirical data — namely, the statements, emotions, and behavior of their patients or clients. The clinical setting, they claim, is a rich source of evidence which cannot be denied just because it does not fit the traditional rigid requirements for standard scientific experiments. This claim is very significant for Christianity and other religions as well; for if it is allowed, it means that the same criteria for what constitutes evidence are equally applicable to the encounters between clergymen and the spiritually starved who seek their guidance.

The 'clinical evidence' of the impact of conversion or spiritual rebirth has often been used to argue the validity of such experiences. Verbal reports (whether autobiographical or by witnesses) and the great joy, wisdom, and effectiveness of the saints constitute some of the major traditional proofs of Christianity. We now hear that such observations, in this kind of setting and relationship, are considered to constitute acceptable scientific evidence.

It is not a satisfactory rebuttal to argue that this kind of evidence should merely be taken as the first stage of data-collecting, after which the more cautious traditional scientific procedure of hypothesis-testing moves in to clean things up. Such a retort fails because (1) the claim offered in the case of self-theory is that this sort of evidence is acceptable by itself; (2) in the case of the self-theorists twenty years have passed without any significant evidence of the more scientific stage developing; and (3) psychiatrists and clinical psychologists have argued recently that the traditional scientific position or paradigm is in principle no longer appropriate. For example, existential psychoanalysis "questions the theoretical root of all major movements in contemporary psychology: the assumption that the study of man can be wholly a natural science." [16]

This shift in theoretical perspective is based on various kinds of arguments to the effect that neither the natural science nor the medical model of psychotherapy is adequate; psychotherapy is interpreted rather as a persuasion process, in which suffering is relieved through the patient's faith in the therapist and by the therapist's warm, sympathetic support combined with experienced application of any of a wide variety of theoretical systems.[17] Although today's systems must have characteristics that will effectively justify the faith of the contemporary patient, the emphasis no longer falls on attempts to "prove the truth" of different theories of psychotherapy. Clinical psychologists used to argue strenuously that their discipline was a bona fide science in order to support its claim to truth (and to help it get millions of tax dollars in support). Today many are describing psychology in categories indistinguishable from those used for religious cures and conversions.

There have been some thoughtful, systematic and scientific attempts to conceptualize and evaluate psychotherapy, but the results are quite modest, especially in terms of the claims of the popularizers.[18]

Little careful and systematic study has been done of the effectiveness and consequences of encounter groups. Rather critical evidence on their effects is presented in what is apparently the first major book on the subject, *Encounter Groups: First Facts*, by Morton Lieberman, Irwin Yalom, and Matthew Miles (1973). A review by Wayne Joosse succinctly summarizes the authors' conclusions regarding the claims typically made for this type of group on the basis of their study:

> The subjects . . . were Stanford University students. This is hardly a sample representative of the general population. Since it was weighted with bright, verbal young people, it favored therapeutic outcomes. The subjects were assigned in an essentially random manner (age, sex, and previous group experience were balanced) to 17 groups representing the ten major theoretical approaches (Gestalt, transactional analysis, Rogerian, etc.). Leaders were selected from among the most highly recommended in northern California, for some reason a particular stronghold of the encounter culture. (This quality leadership again favored misleadingly positive outcomes, for one of the ominous characteristics of the encounter movement is that, in the absence of certification laws, many groups are being "led" by those whose only training and experience is having been in a group before.) . . .
>
> Only about a third of the participants experienced positive changes. Roughly . . . 8% of the total group sustained "significant psychological injury."
>
> "Theoretical orientation" seemed to matter little, though "leader style" did. The more empathetic and supportive leaders ("enlightened paternalism") achieved the greatest number of positive changes while the more aggressive and "charismatic" leaders were correlated with negative outcomes. Distressingly, the leaders themselves were very poor at identifying those who became "casualties," exhibiting instead almost blind faith in themselves and their techniques.[19]

Are We Intrinsically All That Good?

Exactly how extreme are the convictions of the selfists

about the total intrinsic goodness of human nature? The answer is: quite extreme. The popularizers whose books number sales in the millions almost unanimously assume the goodness of the self. They rarely even discuss the problem of that self-expression which leads to exploitation, narcissism, or sadism. The combination of passing over this unpleasant aspect and constantly articulating a clear message of "love and trust yourself and do your own thing" obviously accounts for a good deal of their popularity.

The theorists may hedge on this issue, but not much and not often. Hall and Lindzey, in their well-known text on theories of personality, interpret Maslow's position as definitely implying that "man has an inborn nature which is essentially good and never evil."[20] Remember Fromm's earlier statement that humanist ethics would be untenable if the "dogma of man's innate natural evilness were true." And Rogers' optimism has consistently brought with it the failure to treat systematically such problems as malignant aggression, sadism, and the narcissistic self. Two of Rogers' formal statements about his theory of therapy suggest the limits to which he goes. In his most important theoretical summary Rogers postulates as fundamental processes central to therapy the client's feeling increasingly *"unconditional positive self regard"* and *"experienc*[ing] himself as the *locus of evaluation."*[21] Nowhere in this work does he qualify these principles or identify those people or conditions to which they do not apply. Nor have I found such qualifications in any of his other writings. The encouragement to narcissism, solipsism, and self-indulgence is obvious.

Fromm is much more aware of the problem of evil and its theoretical importance to his position. He has recently devoted a book, *The Anatomy of Human Destructiveness* (1973), to argue his humanist position against rising criticism. In spite of its length, the work fails decisively at defending his particular form of "optimistic" humanism.

There are several major weaknesses in Fromm's argument. First, he divides aggression into two varieties: defensive, useful, "good" aggression; and offensive, malignant aggression. The latter is the only genuine evil, and it is due exclusively to exploitative society and is not part of human nature. The initial difficulty is that the very existence of exploitative societies is not seen as being related to human nature. But there is another equally significant problem with this distinction: in real life few people, if any, can reliably make such a distinction in connection with their own affairs. We have a strong bias to misperceive the legitimate defensive reactions of others as hostile and offensive aggression. This tendency is common even in children as young as one year old, for whom the role of social factors is minimal. As such, this bias is at the heart of much destructive and malignant aggression. A significant part of what is meant by the theological concept of original sin is this bias which warps our judgment and our will.

Second, Fromm attempts to explain the character of certain well-known sadistic and malignant historical figures. His presentation fails to identify any important and unusual childhood environment that could account for the violence and evil they perpetrated as adults. To argue that they were all part of a generally exploitative society is far too vague, since their early home life seems not to have differed from that of millions of others in their own countries and around the world. Fromm's description of the childhood of Hitler reminded me of the childhood of several people I know today. Besides, why should exploitative societies have such effects unless we are predisposed to develop a capacity for violence?

A third major weakness is that Fromm's examples are all taken from extreme historical cases. This is no accident, since it carries with it the suggestion that evil is relatively rare. However congenial this is to Fromm's theory, evil is unfortunately a commonplace experience in the lives of ordinary people. Destructiveness, meanness, and hate are expressed daily in academic departments at universities and theological seminaries, government agencies, business organizations, assembly lines, and homes, in large cities and small towns. Vicious talk, the disguised knife-in-the-back, and the like are acts of which even "nice" people are frequently guilty. The famed banality of evil comes from this ordinariness and pettiness. Violent thoughts and fantasies and pet hatreds are some of our most familiar and pleasure-giving activities. We treasure, even fondle, them. History's great monsters are not necessarily worse than you or I. True, they have had access to great political power with which to further their intentions, and most of us have access to little such power, but the evil is much the same. Pandering to fantasies of violence and revenge is universally a favorite pastime; and when our own internal scenarios begin to bore us we can turn to the immense supply of films and literature specializing in violence.

Fromm fails to appreciate the factor of boredom in stimulating aggressive activity. One of the great appeals of violence and war is that for many it allows escape from tedium by providing an exciting outlet. Psychologist-anthro-pologist Ernest Becker describes historical motives for war in this way:

> Sometimes men went to war out of personal frustration in the tribe, to work off sexual jealousy and grief, or even simple boredom. Life on primitive levels could be monotonous, and warfare was often the main source of new experience, travel, real stimulation.[22]

Boys roaming about in small groups playing at war are obviously having fun, and rarely evidence hatred or true violence in such games. Boredom, or the need for stimulation, as a motivating force has been seriously underrated as a factor in many of today's social problems — juvenile crime, drugs, sexual problems.

Finally, Fromm's biological evidence is extremely un-representative. He ignores evidence for fatal aggression within species; for example, male lions, like many male cats, are frequent killers of their young. This is also true for some male primates. Fromm never discusses the evidence that socially cohesive animals — baboons, for instance — often show both the most intra-group cooperation and the most extra-group aggression. But this selectivity pales beside his omission of recent evolutionary theories of society, in-cluding evolutionary theories of morality and ethics pro-posed by biologists.[23] In its extreme form, the argument of these scientists runs: "The organism does not live for itself, its primary function is not even to reproduce other organisms; it reproduces genes and serves as their temporary carrier." [24] (Recall Bertalanffy's position that ethical principles are verbalized instincts.) One need not accept such radical biological reductionism to see nonetheless that our biological nature provides a theoretical basis for understanding society, one very different from the vague notions proposed by humanistic self-theory. The extreme form of the sociobiologists' argument is that biology determines much or all of our social structure and roles, just as it determines our eye color. For example, many sociobiologists emphasize strict determinism and the intrinsic and untranscendable selfishness of all individuals. Altruism is interpreted as biologically determined and as a disguised form of individual — or, more often, group — selfishness; that is, they make the opposite claim of the humanists, namely that man is totally selfish.*

We shall conclude our presentation of scientific criticism of the selfist positions that human nature is exclusively or even primarily good, and that evil is some kind of mistake by society, with some remarks made recently by social

---

*The biological interpretation of social systems obviously challenges much recent sociological theory. Even some Christian sociologists have argued that man was created by God, but that all society is a human construction, that its structures have no special intrinsic prerogatives, that man has no natural social roles. But the family is a universal cross-cultural unit, and much biological evidence would support the intrinsic nature of the roles it entails. Certainly the family is a basic Christian concept; and thus, in terms of Christian theory, it is a God-given unit and not an arbitrary social fiction. Jesus Christ, like all of us, was born into a family of a father and mother and into the role of child — the son. The social institution of the family is central to Christ's life and teaching — particularly the relation of Jesus to God the Father and his life as an expression of divine sonship. The special importance of his mother, the Virgin Mary, and of the Mother Church are well known. The view of the Christian community as a brotherhood or extended family is also familiar and essential to Christian doctrine. We shall look in detail at selfism and the family in Chapter 7.

psychologist Donald Campbell, president of the American Psychological Association and advocate of evolutionary social and biological interpretations of human society. Campbell sees in contemporary American society a "non-optimal production of underinhibited, overly narcissistic and overly selfish individuals," for which psychology must take considerable blame:

> There is in psychology today a general background assumption that the human impulses provided by biological evolution are right and optimal, both individually and socially, and that repressive or inhibitory moral traditions are wrong. This assumption may now be regarded as scientifically wrong. Psychology, in propagating this background perspective in its teaching of perhaps 80 or 90 percent of college undergraduates, and increasing proportions of high school and elementary school pupils, helps to undermine the retention of what may be extremely valuable social-evolutionary inhibitory systems which we do not yet fully understand.

Specifically, he says, there is "social functionality and psychological validity to the concepts of sin and temptation and of original sin due to human carnal, animal nature."*[25]

---

*Many of the psychologists responding to Campbell's address construed the central moral issue as that of the individual's well-being, expressed through actions rewarding the self, versus society's well-being, obtained by people giving up their liberty to a moral code and becoming altruistic. This is a very low-level representation of the problem. The higher religions claim that through love of God, through transcendent experience, the *individual* is dramatically better off. One important consequence of spiritual transformation is greater altruistic behavior. Thus, in the religious interpretation the individual and society are not in conflict but in *fundamental cooperation.*

Chapter Four

From a Philosophical Point of View

A Question of Definitions

From a philosophical perspective, the most obvious difficulty with selfism is that its proponents fail adequately to define or characterize their central concept — the self. The closest any of them comes to recognition of this problem occurs in the writings of the existentialists; and even then there are severe difficulties, as we shall discuss below. In the case of the American self-theorists, this fundamental issue is essentially passed over. For them the meaning of the concept of the "self" is self-evident. The "I" or "me," as each person experiences it, is accepted at face value as valid. Of course, many examples of selves engaged in actualizing themselves are given, but the examples do not clarify some of the basic difficulties. For example: are there not many and conflicting parts and layers of the self? Certainly such conflict between different self-goals, different ideals, and so forth, is a common experience. If so, which is the "real" self? How does one choose among the various selves? If it is claimed there is only one "true" self, or that the different true selves do not conflict, what is the basis for the claim? How is the true potential of the self recognized? Does the concept of the self not contain a nature or essence which restricts authentic existence and therefore should be rejected? Is the concept of the self not in fact given by society — particularly modern Western society? The self-theorists apparently think not, since they are constantly contrasting the self with society, which is usually seen as the enemy.

Difficulties like these have been raised for years.

Although B. F. Skinner's own position is neither adequate nor consistent, one sympathizes with the objection he pointed out in a 1956 debate with Rogers:

> What evidence is there that a client ever becomes truly *self-directing*? What evidence is there that he ever makes a truly *inner* choice of ideal or goal? Even though the therapist does not do the choosing, even though he encourages "self-actualization" — he is not out of control as long as he holds himself ready to step in when occasion demands — when, for example, the client chooses the goal of becoming a more accomplished liar or murdering his boss. But supposing the therapist does withdraw completely or is no longer necessary — what about all the other forces acting upon the client? Is the self-chosen goal independent of his early ethical and religious training? of the folk wisdom of his group? of the opinions and attitudes of others who are important to him? Surely not.[1]

Rogers has not yet replied.

Does the self spring out of biology? If so, why is our biological nature ignored by self-theorists? Instead, they provide such remarkable descriptions as this by Stevens:

> In the beginning I was one person, knowing nothing but my own experience. Then, I was told things and became two people. . . . In the beginning was I, and I was good. Then came an other I. Outside authority.[2]

Such a summary statement with its total optimism about our basic goodness, with its assumption of a mysterious and undefined "I" expressed in the language of the biblical story of the creation (Stevens' last two lines sound like a parody), and completed with the comforting rationalization that all bad is caused by others is a masterpiece of woolly thinking. Even the obvious question of how other people, all born equally good, managed to develop the ever-present evil social forces and outside authorities is never discussed.*

---

*We should note in passing that the point of accepting evil as intrinsic to human nature is *not* to justify hard-hearted or cynical tolerance of existing evil. Instead it is to include this essential knowledge as part of the starting point for a higher wisdom. A brilliant start on this can be found in Becker's *Escape from Evil*,

A Basic Contradiction

The existential concept of the self, primarily European in origin, has been somewhat more explicitly described. In a scholarly summary MacIntyre writes of the existential self or ego:

> The existentialist individual resembles the Cartesian ego without the *cogito*. Sartre inherited from phenomenology an explicit Cartesianism. In Sartre the individual as the knowing subject is the isolated Cartesian ego; the individual as a moral being is a Kantian man for whom rational first principles have been replaced by criterionless choices. Neither God nor Nature is at hand to render the universe rational and meaningful, and there is no background of socially established and recognized criteria in either knowledge or morals. The individual of existentialism is Descartes's true heir.[3]

MacIntyre's summary reveals that the notion of the existential self presents some major philosophical difficulties. First, such a self — built on the concept of a criterionless choice — appears to be impossible. *A choice based on no criterion is not a choice.* At the least this concept, so contradictory, so bizarre, yet so central to existentialism, should be developed before one accepts the existential self which depends on it. In practice, of course, criteria are accepted by everyone, often unconsciously; and the existential personal philosophy proceeds from them. But a consistent existentialism cannot allow the acceptance of any criteria — particularly unexamined criteria — because of the absurdity of existence. That is, no *a priori* or externally valid principles exist. Not even life itself is intrinsically meaningful.

---

which is a development of the position articulated by William James in the following quotation, which Becker uses as an epigraph:

> There is no doubt that healthy-mindedness is inadequate as a philosophical doctrine, because the evil facts which it positively refuses to account for are a genuine portion of reality; and they may after all be the best key to life's significance, and possibly the only openers of our eyes to the deepest levels of truth.

Thus, a thoroughgoing existentialist could never begin existential life, for the process of choosing can never get started: he cannot get past the problem of the criteria for a first choice. Occasionally, existentialists have recognized this difficulty — as when Camus admits that the only important philosophical question is whether to commit suicide or not. Generally, however, the existentialist violates the principle of complete absurdity and escapes nihilism by assuming that the self, the process of becoming, and some other values (criteria) are valid and not totally meaningless.

This allows the system to get the process of choosing started, but it still leaves open the question of what the actual goal of self-actualization should be. What values and potentials among the many which are available to anyone should I or will I choose? When it comes to defining its famous "authentic self," existentialism is, by definition, no help. In practice, apparently, any social or political philosophy is an acceptable basis for actualization. The lives of the major existentialist writers bear this out dramatically. Martin Heidegger, perhaps the greatest twentieth-century existentialist, was a Nazi for a short period. Karl Jaspers was a liberal. Jean-Paul Sartre has been a Communist or Marxist of sorts for many years. Kierkegaard was a rigid conservative who approved the monarchical repression of the popular liberal movements of 1848. Nietzsche has been interpreted as everything from a fascist to a tormented humanist to an anti-Christ.[4]

This problem of the ethical neutrality of existentialism and of much of the theory underlying American selfism has been obscured by the almost unanimous liberal humanism of the American self-theorists. But there is no reason intrinsic to self-theory that it should be associated with liberal humanist values. That it generally has been so far is due to its (usually unacknowledged) incorporation of assumptions and values from the Judeo-Christian heritage of the American theorists and the dominant liberal or socialist Western intellectual community of the last generation. As America moves into a different, no doubt more turbulent political and intellectual climate, the heterogeneity of those positions which are seen as consistent with selfism will become clear. Evidence suggesting that this has already begun, as shown in recent trends toward extreme self-indulgence, has already been noted and will be discussed further in the next chapters.

Let us look more closely at some of the major existential assumptions and the internal contradictions and difficulties they create. Existentialists accept the existence of the self (*Eigenwelt*), but like the American selfists they never develop a theory of how the self is conditioned by innate biological factors. They also appear to overlook the way in which the existential self is the product of a very particular modern Western society. Because of this two-fold failure to work out how social and innate mental factors affect the self, the arena within which the existential self operates is substantially unspecified. Clearly such factors must condition the "authentic existential self." Without this knowledge, however, the quest for authenticity is so ambiguous as to be fatuous.

For example, because you did not choose them, all of the following — and many more — are not authentic: your age, sex, race, nationality, language, your unconscious personality traits (both the bad and the good ones), your passionate (or calm) temperament, your health, memory, height, weight, intelligence, quality of voice, nice (or bad) teeth, shape of nose, complexion, eye color, and so on. Relentlessly, layer after layer of the inauthentic you is stripped away until a self results which is like a totally peeled onion, of which all that remains is the pure spiritual power of life — in religious terms, the soul. Most of today's existential selfists stop long before, at some inauthentic level; but those few who follow the logic out leave science behind and end in religious language often indistinguishable from the traditional idea of the soul.

Another major problem stems from the fact that existentialism has accepted "reason" — that is, logic, mathematics, and scientific inference — as an essential component of everyone's mental life. The *a priori* existence of reason provides evidence that at least one part of a person's existence — namely, his reason — already has an essence or nature; and this essence precedes the self's existence. Furthermore, the process of reasoning is central to our choices, by which (according to existentialism) our nature is developed. That is, reason has a nature which is present at the start of our existence and it is through the operation of this *a priori* activity that decisions are taken and hence our nature (essence) as individuals develops. Therefore, to a significant degree, the essence of the self proceeds from the essence of rationality. The selfists' neglect of how reason precedes and determines the decisions involved in "choosing" the so-called authentic self can be seen as part of their tendency to ignore all biological or innate properties of man.

Ethical and Scientific Misrepresentations

A final, serious criticism along philosophical lines must address selfism's common tendency to represent itself as both a science and an ethic. The claim that self-theory is a science is invalid by any useful meaning of the term "science," since humanist definitions no longer distinguish psychology and psychotherapy from religion, political ideology, and ethics. Yet, by keeping the name "psychology," which has been represented as a science for decades, by being taught by psychologists (that is, experts) in countless university classes, and by vaguely suggesting ways in which self-theory might be tested, selfism has falsely benefited from the prestige and generally acknowledged special truth value accorded to any science.

A related weakness is the tendency of selfists to imply that psychology as a science has somehow verified the values of secular humanism found in self-theory. The proponents of selfism are generally quite aware of the ethical character of their system. Indeed, they argue cogently that therapeutic psychology cannot possibly operate without values. This position is widely accepted by most thoughtful people today. But how do you demonstrate scientifically the intrinsic goodness of the self, the moral desirability of an "actualizing," "experiencing-in-the-present," "becoming-creative" self?

Obviously, such values have not been scientifically verified. At present there is no satisfactory evidence that science can verify any value. Yet, the aura of authority which psychology has derived from its scientific status is often used by those teaching selfism to imply that its concepts and values somehow have or approach a scientific truth status.

Here I speak from considerable personal experience. As a student I sat in many classes in which, a few weeks after listening to aggressive talk about psychology as "the science of behavior" or "the scientific study of mind," I heard lectures on "self-actualization" and "encounter group processes and goals." No questions were raised about whether the initial arguments for psychology's scientific status still held. As a young assistant professor during the 1960s I taught courses on motivation and personality, in which lectures on the theories of Maslow, Fromm, and Rogers followed close after lectures on instinctual, hormonal, and biochemical interpretations of motivation. All of this was and still is typical of the curriculum in the so-called scientific study of motivation and personality. However, had I also lectured on Christian interpretations of human motivation as providing a reasonable, observationally grounded synthesis of the problems of the self, it would have been seen — and would be seen today — as an arbitrary and unacceptable intrusion of religion into science.

Chapter Five

Selfism and Today's Society

A Creed for the Youth Culture

As we have already suggested, a serious difficulty with selfism is that while it locates many psychologically important events in society, it never comes to grips with the question of who or what is responsible for society. This issue can be seen as particularly acute when these theorists' own actions — writing books, running groups, and so forth — are integral parts of the same society they attack. Indeed, their favorite procedure for debunking earlier belief systems — calling them rationalizations and justifications of the social powers existing at the time they were formulated — can be turned with great effect on Fromm, Rogers, and Maslow. It is certainly no accident that self-growth emerged as a value in American society when it was experiencing economic expansion on a scale unprecedented in human history, bringing great wealth to more people than ever before. Nowhere was this heady growth more evident than in American colleges and universities, which filled with more and more young people experiencing the usual growth in interpersonal relationships and intellectual development that characterize people in their late teens and early twenties. What more natural belief-system could there be than selfism — with its application of a kind of Chamber of Commerce economic growth philosophy to mental life — in a society of burgeoning wealth which had long trumpeted the supreme value of the individual and the intrinsic value of change?

Fromm has criticized what he sees as childish philosophical elements in the life and dogma of medieval Christianity. But if the Middle Ages were childish, and if the Renaissance and Reformation (as Erikson says of Luther's revolt in particular) were similar to *early* adolescent rebellion,[1] it begins to look as though the last two centuries may be likened to a *late* adolescent identity crisis, a period when a kind of teen-age or college-age philosophy is prevalent. People with such a world-view are characterized by a narrow rationalism, on the basis of which they attack the beliefs of their childhood; by rebellion as a routine attitude; and by extreme preoccupation with sex.

The pose of rebellion, the clichés of disobedience and of hostility to hierarchy and authority that have been unchallenged for years in the modern world, are wearing out. The time has come for a child*like* philosophy to reassert its superiority to an adolescent one. A wise yet childlike way of life is how many of the highest religions and philosophies have been described. Such wisdom is, of course, far from identical with the actual world-view of children. Nevertheless, many important attitudes and beliefs of childhood are incorporated therein. There do not appear to be any forms of wisdom that enshrine the beliefs or behavior of youth.

Selfism and Language

A distressing symptom of the spread of selfist ideas throughout our culture has been its effect on everyday linguistic expression. In conversation and in students' papers it has become common for "I feel" to be substituted for "I know" or "I think" — for example: "I *feel* that the conclusions were not justified." A Catholic brochure on the life of Mother Elizabeth Seton, recently canonized as the first American-born saint, features in bold letters on its cover: "To her world she brought her self." It is not, of course, "her world," nor did she bring "her self" in anything like the completely autonomous way suggested by the copy-writer. More religious, far less selfist, would be the statement "To God's world she gave herself." The lyrics of the song "Oklahoma," written a generation ago, "We belong to the land and the land we belong to is grand," contrast with the recent popular but disturbingly possessive words of "This land is your land, this land is my land, from California to the New York Island." The passive idea of being possessed by the land is typical of all people who are deeply attached to land and nature; the attitude disclosed by the active "my land" is, by contrast, very modern and selfist.

C. FitzSimons Allison makes this point about the active and passive voice with special clarity in two instances. He reports that Albert Einstein once said in a conversation with Robert Oppenheimer:

> "When it has been once given to you to do something rather reasonable, forever afterwards your work and life are a little strange." This passive voice [Allison remarks], ". . . when it has once been given," has been used by extraordinarily creative persons since pagan times in exploring the source or genesis of their creativity. But the tide of modern times is going in the opposite direction. . . .[2]

In the other instance Allison discusses a *National Geographic* report in which Alan Villiers retraced Darwin's famous voyage on the *Beagle*. Allison notes that:

> In his narrative Villiers introduces a number of quotations from Darwin's diary. What strikes the reader is the difference in perspective between Darwin and Villiers. The former speaks of the ocean that "was here spread out," one species of bird "had been taken and modified for different ends," searching for the grand scheme "on which organized beings have been created," a special variety "had been modified for different ends." Villiers, a faithful representative of our age with its characteristic *hubris*, infers from Darwin's findings that all change, modification, and design is from within creation, autogenous, autonomous. He writes: "No wonder the local cormorant *has evolved* into a flightless bird. . . ."[3]

Selfism's active voice emphasis is contrasted by Allison with Christian worship, which "against all forms of idolatry is always and primarily rendered in the passive voice, in the expectancy and primacy of God's action and Word. In such worship we do not invent values but discern them. We do not fashion our own identities but we are shaped and refashioned by the Spirit of God. Abraham, Moses, the prophets, and the disciples were all called. God's word came to them and their work was a response."[4]

Psychology for a Consumer Society

Rogers describes self-theory and encounter groups as radical, but their ready acceptance by millions of people makes this claim shallow. Selfism is in fact the perfect consumer philosophy, ideally suited for those with money and leisure. It is especially good for people who consume services like travel and fashion. Early consumer advertising and the philosophy behind it aimed at selling *things*. Today's selfist emphasis, reflecting a later stage in consumer philosophy, is used to sell *services* and *activities*: that is, life-styles.

The material success of the contemporary economy underlies many of the assumptions which emerge in the selfists' writings. Recall Fromm's statement that man is justifiably proud of modern science and technology. Recall, too, his claim, now seen as naive, that modern man has in theory solved the problem of economic production. Fromm may criticize the aggressive, competitive, and acquisitive character of the "marketing" personality produced by modern capitalism, but the selfist personality is in fact a creation of the material and social conditions of a rich economy in which serious scarcity is (or at least was) a thing of the past. Rogers, for example, assumes that the general trend of human relationships found in contemporary America (especially the Los Angeles area), which is dependent on modern inventions and the associated urban economy, will continue on the same trajectory.[5] Typically Rogers views contemporary changes in traditional personal relationships as progressive. He cites with some enthusiasm his projections that by the year 2000 there will be truly effective computerized matching of couples, sex will have almost completely lost its role in procreation (that sex has major spiritual and religious significance is not acknowledged), effective long-term birth control techniques will be commonplace, so that lasting infertility of adolescents and marriages of various degrees of impermanence will be common.[6] He concludes his discussion of partnership with an exhortation:

> Any modern industry is judged in part by the size of its investment in R and D — research and development. It is recognized that a company cannot succeed unless it is eliminating past failures, exploring new possibilities, studying new materials for its products . . . [and is] supported by endless funds.
>
> Experimentation is central to all technological advances, no matter how many traditions it overthrows. It is not only accepted, but financed and admired by the public. Change is the name of the game, and this is known and accepted by almost everyone. . . .

Then he turns to the particular subject of the book:

> Marriage and the nuclear family constitute a failing institution, a failing way of life. No one would argue that these have been highly successful. We need laboratories, experiments, attempts to avoid repeating past failures, exploration into new approaches.[7]

We shall bypass for now the religious and ethical issues raised by passages like this. Nor shall we scrutinize the assumptions made about the almost universal acceptance and admiration of modern technology. Let us look briefly at some of the economic assumptions of Rogers' position. Clearly he accepts and admires the processes central to the modern economy, with its constant advance derived from research and supported by "endless funds" from an enthusiastic public. The arguments of no-growth and negative-growth economists, the ecologically grounded reservations about big cities and modern technology, the growing rational hostility to modern agriculture and big business — all are simply ignored.[8] An important example of the type of criticism which is utterly disregarded by the selfists is the intelligent and increasingly influential economic argument for a return to a simpler and less industrial society made by the Christian economist E. F. Schumacher.[9] Many others make out a similar case. Any such return to an environment resembling pre-industrial society would suggest that social values and interpersonal relations might also become similar to those in pre-industrial society. In any case values and relationships in the future are unlikely to resemble a more extreme extension of those found today. The selfists, by assuming business as usual, inadvertently acknowledge the dependence of much of their psychology on what many now see as a peculiar situation — the last stages of a late industrial urban economy, which has already begun to collapse.

It certainly proved convenient that just as Western economies began to need consumers there developed an ideology hostile to discipline, to obedience, and to the delaying of gratification. Selfism's clear advocacy of experience *now*, and not inhibiting or repressing, was a boon to the advertising industry, which was finding that the returns on appeals to status and product quality were diminishing. Most of the short expressions and catch-words of self-theory make excellent advertising copy: *Do it now! Have a new experience! Honor thyself!*

Some of the clearest examples of selfist jargon in advertising are found in the pages of the popular magazines oriented to educated affluent consumers — magazines like *Playboy, Penthouse,* and *Psychology Today.* Some representative recent copy for advertisements in *Psychology Today* ran:

> I LOVE ME. I am not conceited. I'm just a good friend to myself. And I like to do whatever makes me feel good. . . .
>
> . . . We live by a certain philosophy: We try to make our dreams come true today, instead of waiting for tomorrow. But before you can do good things for yourself, you have to know yourself. . . . You need self-knowledge before you can have self-satisfaction. Think about it.[10]

It is difficult to distinguish in these magazines between editorial philosophy and advertising copy.

That much of selfism is dependent on a broad base of economic prosperity has been driven home in the last few years by inflation and recession. It has become very hard to actualize oneself at today's prices.

The call to self-indulgent appropriation of the benefits

of prosperity is not always expressed as crudely as it is in these advertisements. Often it is cloaked by high-sounding motives. For instance, developing people's "creative potential" has been a standard goal for educators as well as psychologists for many years now. What is meant by creativity is that the adult or child express his potential, assumed to be intrinsically good (bad potential does not exist). They do not mean accomplishing anything of genuine creative significance.* This *worship* of creativity seems to be an outgrowth of the Romanticism of the nineteenth century. What was worshiped then was the rare 'god' categorizable as the Genius. Gradually the "elitist" valuing of the Genius was transformed by American society into the inflated but

---

*One reader, a theologian, criticized this last comment as extreme, noting that the people involved in these "creative" activities would certainly disagree with the claim that such activities have no merit. His reaction was based on the fact that the participants developing their "creative potential" *feel* rewarded.

For a Christian, however, all creativity has its origin in God; and to claim that an individual human is really creative is either silly or blasphemous. A person can express his individual capacity in a creative fashion only by aligning himself with God's will. Real creativity requires a soul cooperating with God — a soul who becomes God's loving agent in all its activity however mundane. There is certainly no Christian basis for the massive egos so common in the modern artist. There is an important Christian valuing of creativity, but the creative act is viewed as a gift from God, in its greatest sense, the gift of life for man and all living creatures and the gift of existence to nonliving things.

As secular humanism developed, especially in the nineteenth century, the expression "creative" began to be applied to great artists or thinkers — those who gave others music, paintings, scientific theory. The initial divine aspect (present even in pre-Christian time) has long since dropped out, and now even the idea that creativity involves giving something to others is gone. Today in the secular world creativity is simply a gift from the self *to* the self, it has degenerated into a synonym for any form of personal pleasure without reference to others. I recently heard a lecturer on sexual behavior seriously argue for "creative masturbation."

Hence, the original claim is accurate: within the narcissistic logic of selfism, being "creative" does not mean doing anything of

comforting belief that the sacred creative self was centered in everyone. Our egos are all as worthy of worship as that of the Genius. Naturally, the supporting values of rebellion and defiant independence have been brought in as equally ideal for all of us. In the spread of this popular and flattering belief creativity has been turned into a rationale for self-indulgence.

Recently Robert Heilbroner has cogently and powerfully argued the chilling case for the inevitability of economic and political disasters that will result in a new society in which sheer survival will be the primary goal. In considering the forecast of this new communal, much more agricultural and perhaps even monastic society, Heilbroner writes:

> Talleyrand once remarked that only those who had lived in the *ancien régime* could know what *"les douceurs de la vie"* could be. He was referring to the *douceurs* of a court in which elegance and extravagance knew no bounds, and in which the wealthy and highly placed could indulge their whims and caprices with an abandon that we can only look back upon with the mixed feelings with which we regard the indulgence of all infantile desires.
>
> In our period of history, however, it may well be that the threatened *douceurs* are those of an intellectual milieu in which the most extravagant and heretical thoughts can be uttered. . . . Indeed, might not the people of such a threatened society look upon the "self-indulgence" of unfettered intellectual expression with much the same mixed feelings that we hold with respect to the ways of a vanished aristocracy — a way of life no doubt agreeable to the few who benefited from it, but of no concern, or even of actual disservice, to the vast majority?[11]

Our thesis is that self-actualization is a more generic

genuine significance. In fact, a good case could be made for the net *negative* contribution to social, spiritual and religious life by training in creativity and self-actualization. Many people today have such high opinions of their "creative potential" that they prefer welfare to work at available but humble jobs — that is, jobs below their self-defined level of worth. Creativity programs have become schools for inordinate pride.

term for what Heilbroner refers to as "self-indulgence" and the uttering of "extravagant and heretical thoughts." We need *not* assume the cataclysms and consequent future of Heilbroner and others who have made similar predictions to appreciate how great is the wealth needed for a society to provide for the physical conditions of self-actualization for even a small proportion of its people. Americans forget that they are, in terms of wealth, the upper-upper class of the world. The college campuses and youth culture in the United States in the last two decades have shown all the frivolity and arrogance of the courts of the *ancien régime*. Like the French court, but on a larger scale, there has been in them little awareness of the fragile basis for the prosperity being enjoyed and of its dependence on people living far away. Instead it is seriously proposed that self-actualization be a universal ethic for a future that is likely to raise the question of sheer survival. By comparison, "Let them eat cake" shines as a statement of compassionate realism.

Chapter Six

Selfism and Christianity: Historical Antecedents

In the next three chapters we shall take up an explicitly Christian analysis and criticism of humanistic self-theories. We shall begin the process in this chapter with a documentation of some of the important historical relationships between the two faiths.

Feuerbach

The popularizers of selfism, as far as I have been able to discover, never refer to the historical origins of their ideas. Thus they give the impression — so typical of American enthusiasm — that their ideas are genuinely new, the result of recent and extraordinary changes in technology and society.* What is in fact new in modern selfism is not its more than century-old system of ideas, but the large number of people who now endorse it. Some of the particular applications and social consequences of selfism as discussed above are of recent origin as well.

The popularizers often acknowledge their theoretical debt to Rogers and to Maslow, less often to May and Fromm.

---

*This is hardly the only case in which an idea originating in Europe has had its first large-scale application in America. Later, the large-scale effects often cross to Europe and are called Americanization. For example, a European invents the automobile, the United States creates the automobile society, which is then exported back to Europe.

But the writings of Rogers and Maslow show only the vaguest understanding of the work of the earlier theorists from whom their positions derive. May, no doubt because of his experience and contacts in Europe, is historically somewhat more informed, while Fromm is by far the most scholarly and aware of his debt to nineteenth-century European thought, although even he neglects the central importance of Feuerbach to the humanist theory of the self.

Despite the ahistorical character and secular trappings of contemporary self-theories, their origins are nonetheless closely connected to Christianity, frequently in a hostile way. Consequently, a brief review of these important historical connections will prepare for our explicitly Christian criticism in later chapters.

The most important direct source for today's humanistic selfism is Ludwig Feuerbach's *The Essence of Christianity*. First published in 1841, revised in 1843, this work by a left-wing follower of Hegel became widely known for its influential attack on Christianity. Friedrich Engels described his response to the book: "One must himself have experienced the liberating effect of this book to get an idea of it. Enthusiasm was general; we all became at once Feuerbachians."[1] Among other later thinkers whose ideas about religion were directly or indirectly affected by Feuerbach were Marx, Nietzsche, Huxley, John Stuart Mill, Freud, and Dewey. The tradition of Marx, Nietzsche, and Freud leads to Fromm and May; that of Mill, Huxley, and Dewey connects directly to Rogers and Maslow.

The book consists of an argument against both the divinity of Christ and the existence of God, with the general premise that all theology be resolved into anthropology. Some representative quotations make clear the nature of Feuerbach's arguments and their similarity to those of today's self-theorists:

> Though theology does not realize it, man, by positing Christ as the God incarnate, has proclaimed that man's selfless love for humanity constitutes salvation. . . .
>
> . . . Therefore we ought to strive toward godliness, for in and through God man aims at his true self.

> . . . the historical progress of religion consists in this:
> that which during an earlier stage of religion was regarded
> as something objective is now recognized as something sub-
> jective, so that which was formerly viewed and worshipped as
> God is now recognized as something human.
>
> But that which in religion ranks first — namely, God — is,
> as I have shown, in truth and reality something second; for
> God is merely the projected essence of Man.
>
> What, therefore, ranks second in religion — namely, Man
> — that must be proclaimed the first and recognized as the
> first.
>
> If the nature of Man is man's Highest Being, if to be human
> is his highest existence, then man's love for Man must in
> practice become the first and highest law. Homo homini
> Deus est — man's God is MAN. This is the highest law of
> ethics. THIS IS THE TURNING POINT OF WORLD HISTORY.[2]

Engels and Marx considered Feuerbach's conception of
man much too abstract and speculative, and they subse-
quently developed their familiar economic and political
interpretation of human nature. Yet Marx acknowledges the
debt he owes Feuerbach for his "dissolution of the religious
world into its secular basis. . . . Feuerbach resolves the
religious essence into the human."[3] It is interesting in this
connection that Feuerbach first said, "Religion is as bad as
opium,"[4] a comparison later echoed by Marx in his famous
attack on religion.

Feuerbach's interpersonal interpretation of man's nature
is present in such statements as "the essence of man is
contained only in community, in the unity of man with man
— a unity which however is founded only on the reality of
the differences between I and thou."[5] The resonance here
with Fromm — and even Martin Buber — is obvious. Although a detailed examination of the origins of modern self-
theory and secular humanism lies beyond the scope of our
treatment here, the case of Feuerbach indicates that in good
measure today's humanist self-theories represent reformula-
tions and extensions of the theses of earlier thinkers who
were explicitly anti-Christian. The relatively derivative
character of contemporary self-theory would be clearer if
the hundred years between Feuerbach and the American

theories were investigated. One important intervening humanism, for instance, is that of the century-old Ethical Culture Society.[6]

Fosdick and Peale

By contrast, a surprising pair of immediate precursors of selfist thought in the United States were popular Protestant ministers during the period from 1920 to the mid-1950s, neither of whom is taken very seriously as a theorist: Harry Emerson Fosdick and Norman Vincent Peale.

Fosdick, a writer and preacher of wide influence, developed his ideas in New York City in the 1920s, 30s, and 40s — the formative place and period for most of American self-theory. A champion of liberal Protestant theology, he was also associated with Union Theological Seminary. We shall look at three of Fosdick's books which nicely summarize the development of his brand of self-theory. Not only are the basic ideas that he combined to create his theory interesting, but of even greater interest is the fact that these ideas were popular in a liberal Christian context *before* being widely published in the purely secular literature of psychology. That is, the first *popular* expression of such notions as "self-realization," "becoming a real person," and the like appears to have occurred in New York's Protestant pulpits.

The first book important for a summary of Fosdick's self-theory is *Christianity and Progress,* published in 1922. In a short preface Fosdick sets the tone for the book by describing the progress of the nineteenth century with the following words of Renan: "the substitution of the category of *becoming* for *being,* of the conception of relativity for that of the absolute, of movement for immobility."[7] The book itself develops this theme by assuming that the idea of progress — in both the material and social senses — had not only become the dominant but the correct view of history. Fosdick argues that Christianity is intrinsically a progressive religion, and that therefore modern progress and Christianity are natural partners. By implication, Christianity is the religion of becoming, of relativity, of movement. The dangers of complacent optimism or of too simple a trust in progress are acknowledged, but the link of Christianity to dynamic progress is Fosdick's central message in this work.

Ten years later, in *As I See Religion*, Fosdick answers the question, What is Christianity? "The divine origin, spiritual nature, infinite worth, and endless possibilities" of each "personality," he tells us, with its "power of intellect, creative hope and love" and "promise of development" constitute the "essential genius" of Christianity.[8] That is, the individual personality with all its promise for creative development is the *central* Christian concept. Given Fosdick's emphasis on the two ideas of progress and personality, one is hardly surprised that this line of thinking evolved by 1943 into a theoretical position much like today's selfism. Even the title of this third, and extremely popular book, *On Being a Real Person*, brings to mind the current situation, for Rogers entitled his most popular work *On Becoming a Person* (1961).

Before we summarize Fosdick's position briefly, we may note how his ideas developed. In the introduction Fosdick chronicles his deepening involvement over the years in religious counseling, mental health, and psychiatry. He addresses the book partly to ministers who face similar counseling problems but primarily to readers like those people who have come to him for help. *On Being a Real Person* is obviously an early variety of the psychological "self-help" book, and the author emphasizes his indebtedness to the many psychiatrists, neurologists, and psychological counselors who helped him over the years.

Fosdick begins, "The central business of every human being is to be a real person." This ideal of a "real person" he bases on a personality theory which is presented as follows: "To be a person is to be engaged in a perpetual process of becoming. . . . The basic urge of the human organism is toward wholeness. The primary command of our being is, Get yourself together, and the fundamental sin is to be chaotic and unfocused. . . . When at last maturity is reached . . . , the whole organism can be drawn together into that 'acme of integration' which appears in creative work." Fosdick also makes the important observation that "in modern psychological parlance the word 'integration' has taken the place of the religious word 'salvation.' "[9] Integration, according to Fosdick, derives from self-discovery, self-acceptance, and self-love. It is expressed in creative activity and general well-being.

Fosdick's position contains Christian and religious vestiges, but in much of his theory of personality the ideas are thoroughly anti-Christian and difficult to distinguish from those of today's psychological self-theorists, especially Rogers. Indeed, one of the concepts Fosdick stresses is the discrepancy between a person's ideal self and his perceived or actual self. This discrepancy he views as the major cause of anxiety and fear. Self-acceptance and self-love will, he argues, remove this dysfunctional anxiety and then, through integrated growing, a person can become his real self. Rogers is also known for his emphasis on the discrepancy between the actual and ideal self, but Fosdick in many ways preceded him on this issue.[10]

Where Fosdick got the concepts of self-realization, becoming, and integration is not clear. They were probably very much in the intellectual atmosphere in the period 1925-1945. Psychologists most frequently cited in *On Being a Real Person* are Alfred Adler, Gordon Allport, William James, and Carl Jung. Adler first introduced the notion of the "creative self," and thus he is probably an important direct influence. It may be relevant that Adler lost his ties with his Jewish background and in 1904 joined the Protestant church. Apparently he did this because he wanted to be part of a universal religion not restricted to a single ethnic group. There is no evidence of actual religious experience — much less a conversion — just an ethical and philosophical compatibility. Ellenberger reports that Adler "found it worthwhile to have discussions with a Protestant minister. . . . Adler acknowledged that both had much in common in the ideals they pursued, though one remained in the field of science and the other in that of faith."[11]

William James is often interpreted as setting the stage for today's self- and ego-theories, but the dynamic emphasis on becoming and integration is not especially Jamesian.

Gordon Allport is known for self-realization concepts, but the publications in which he expounded them came years after Fosdick's book. Allport's *Personality: A Psychological Interpretation* (1937) is referred to by Fosdick several times, and this work is suggestive of such dynamic concepts.

Regardless of these influences, Fosdick was one of the earlier synthesizers of an interesting self-theory, and apparently he is the first by many years to make a self-theory the major thesis of a widely *popular* book — *On Being a Real Person* is still in print, in its 29th hardcover printing.

Norman Vincent Peale is primarily interested in case histories that demonstrate his dynamic "Positive Thinking" approach to life's problems. Still, he has to operate with a theory of personality, and, in spite of Christian components, this theory for Peale is essentially selfist in character. As early as 1937 Peale wrote: "The greatest day in any individual's life is when he begins for the first time to realize himself."[12] This assumption that self-realization is a central principle of personality is a constant in Peale's books throughout the next thirty years. He began *The Power of Positive Thinking* (1952) with "Believe in *yourself!* Have faith in *your* abilities! . . . self-confidence leads to self-realization and successful achievement."

Despite the frequent references to Scripture and Christian teaching (which give the book what wisdom it has), the overriding message and basis for its popularity is Peale's Christian rationalization of self-realization. Its selfist character shines through its chapter titles: "How to Create Your Own Happiness"; "Expect the Best and Get It." This emphasis on having faith in the self reduces God to a useful servant of the individual in his quest for personal goals ("How to Draw Upon That Higher Power"). Many of Peale's case histories purport to demonstrate how prayer and faith have enabled someone to win in some competition or to gain business success.

Peale has generally been ignored as a thinker since his work is not especially scholarly. Yet, the content and popularity of his message parallel that of Fosdick and of many of today's secular self-help writers. Most of his books are now available in paperback, and they are widely featured in "self-help" sections of bookstores. Peale's formative period was also the 1930s and 40s in the liberal Protestant atmosphere of New York City. Like Fosdick he was strongly influenced by psychology, and his extensive experience in pastoral counseling led to occasional co-authoring with psychiatrist Smiley Blanton.[13]

To try to explain the appearance of an immensely popular humanist selfism in harmony with liberal Protestantism is a complex and interesting historical problem. As a rough approximation, what seems to have happened is that with the rise of secular ideas and values, especially psychological theories, the basic Christian concept of the unique importance of the self was stripped of its theological justification. Such traditional spiritual concepts as those which anchored the Christian self in experiences like prayer, contemplation, obedience, and mysticism — in faith — became so weak in mainline twentieth-century Protestantism as to be of little significance. The notion of pride as the fundamental sin — along with greed, envy, and the others — yielded to the belief that "the fundamental sin is to be chaotic, and unfocused." The importance of the individual self was also enhanced by the political rationale of democracy and the popular secular tradition. However, a higher justification of the self required a more personal and less social and political rationale; and selfist humanism came in to provide the necessary "theory." Recall Fosdick's observation that integration and self-realization had replaced salvation.

The period of Fosdick and Peale was one of transition, in which a generation of faltering Christians, bored with and skeptical of basic Christian theology and ignorant of spiritual life, accepted an increasingly humanist notion of the self which had been dressed up with superficial Christian language and concepts. The emergence of the huge — and much more secularized — post-World War II generation signaled a new population that was ready for a pure selfism no longer associated with what was seen as the Christian preachiness of their parents' generation. In the United States the crucible for this transformation was the nation's educational system, as we shall discuss more fully below.

Pietism

A final historical precedent is significant: the similarity documented by Thomas Oden of encounter groups to the Christian pietism and Jewish Hasidism of the eighteenth and nineteenth centuries.[14] Modern Protestant pietism originated in the seventeenth century and became a very significant religious and social phenomenon in the eighteenth and nineteenth centuries. In its various manifestations there was an emphasis on intense emotional response, usually occurring in small groups but sometimes involving larger revival meetings. Pietism was a reaction against the arid, intellectualistic, authoritarian forms which Lutheran, Anglican, and Jewish established religions had taken. The period of its rise was, like our own day, a time of change and mobility, particularly on the American frontier. John Wesley's Methodist pietism is perhaps the best known, but there were many other forms, including Quakers, Shakers, the Harmony Community, and the Oneida Community. Communitarian societies were fairly common among the pietists, which suggests a similarity with today's "encounter" culture that Oden does not develop.

Oden thoroughly documents major similarities between pietism and encounter groups — the small group format, a zealous pursuit of honesty, a focus on "here and now" experiencing, interpersonal intimacy, frequent long and intensive meetings (religious revivals and encounter group marathons). Oden presents the evidence for these factors through an extensive series of quotations from the literature of both groups. The following citations from pietist sources highlight similarities with encounter group psychology.

> They began to bear one another's burdens, and naturally to "care for each other." As they had daily a more intimate acquaintance with, so they had a more endearing affection for, each other. Wesley, 1748.

> Let your expressions be clear and definite, pointed and brief having reference to your present experience. Newstead, 1843.

Beware of resting in past experience. Newstead, 1843.

Self-examination, severe, thorough, impartial. The class meeting will be productive of but little real, lasting benefit without this. Rosser, 1855.[15]

Oden's conclusion that the encounter group culture is a demythologized, secularized Judeo-Christian theology is consistent with the case we have presented here. He goes on to develop a theological interpretation of encounter group ideology which is important and generally convincing. He argues that the underlying basic questions of encounter theology (for our purposes, read "selfist" theology) are:

I	II	III
What are the limits of my being that frustrate my self-actualization?	What possibilities are open for deliverance from my predicament?	How can I actualize these possibilities in order to become more fulfilled?

This threefold sequence, which underlies effective psychotherapy regardless of theoretical orientation, is expressed in Christian worship in the form of three acts:

I	II	III
Confession	Thanksgiving	Commitment

Some alternative Christian ways of representing this structure are: bondage → deliverance → mission; sin → grace → responsibility; the human predicament → the gospel → the life of faith.[16]

Oden's analysis provides another view of the religious character of selfism and raises the question of the particular historical relationship that existed between pietism and encounter ideas. Although the historical development of pietism and its connection to encounter groups and modern selfism needs to be researched more thoroughly, Oden has provided enough information to negate decisively Carl Rogers' claim that encounter groups are a social invention of this century.

The Special Case of Carl Rogers

Of the major self-theorists Carl Rogers has probably had

greatest impact. Robert Sollod, a clinical psychologist, contends that from an intellectual point of view Rogers is not a great innovator of ideas so much as "the leader of a movement in which certain ideas are developed, promulgated, and explored under his aegis."[17] Undeniably, however, Rogers' ideas have been assimilated into the mainstream of American psychology, counseling, and education; and many young people have been drawn to encounter groups. Consequently, it is appropriate to single him out for special attention at this point, beginning with a short historical analysis of the origins of his ideas and concluding with a discussion of the significant religious character of Rogerian psychology.

Rogers, in the description of his professional and personal development, recounts a revealing event which occurred while he was still a student at Union Theological Seminary:

> A group of us felt that ideas were being fed to us whereas we wished primarily to explore our own questions and doubts and find out where they led. We petitioned the administration that we be allowed to set up a seminar for credit, a seminar with no instructor, where the curriculum would be composed of our own questions. . . .[18]

He goes on to say that the only restriction was that, in the interests of the institution,

> a young instructor was to sit in on the seminar but would take no part in it unless we wished him to be active. . . . The majority of the members of that group in thinking their way through the questions they had raised thought themselves right out of religious work. I was one. I felt that questions as to the meaning of life, and the possibility of the constructive improvement of life for individuals would probably always interest me, but I could not work in a field where I would be required to believe in some specified religious doctrine. My beliefs had already changed tremendously and might continue to change. It seemed to me it would be a horrible thing to *have* to profess a set of beliefs, in order to remain in one's profession. I wanted to find a field in which I could be sure my freedom of thought would not be limited.

Sollod points out that the preceding paragraph prefigures — from a time before he became a psychologist — many of the major directions of Rogers' future thinking. Notice the emphasis on groups, the negative attitude toward authority and education as traditionally practiced, the desire that individuals find their own beliefs — which, it is assumed, will result in continually changing beliefs throughout life. There is also the assumption that change is good and that it leads away from tradition, authority, and religion. Rogers' personal move away from Christianity has remained as an implicit anti-religious model in his subsequent writings.

In spite of his distaste for fixed doctrines Rogers is a clear example of one who holds firmly to the fixed dogma that modern knowledge has rendered Christianity and other traditional religions permanently out of date. A corollary of this doctrine, rigidly held in much of the contemporary academic world, particularly by social scientists, is that the intelligent believer will sooner or later rebel from the faith. Indeed, on the basis of my personal experience, dating from the middle 1950s to the present, I would say that the abandonment of one's "religious background" is *reliably* assumed to be a rational consequence of getting an education, particularly in graduate schools. The basis for this assumption, of course, never comes under the sort of systematic investigation, motivated by an honest quest for understanding spiritual or religious truth, which one might expect from the university, given the lofty ideals it professes. In brief, the anti-religious prejudice expressed by Rogers in the passage quoted above was and still is a commonplace in the academic world.

If Rogers' early and rather intellectual "encounter group" experience was the kernel from which much of his later thought grew, where did he get the conceptual framework that was to provide adequate intellectual content for his position? Rogers suggests the link by stating that after he crossed the street from Union Seminary to Columbia Teachers College he came under the strong influence of the famous educator William H. Kilpatrick, an advocate of Dewey's philosophy, whom Rogers describes as "a great teacher."[19] The influence of Dewey on Rogers through the medium of Kilpatrick must have been very strong. Sollod notes the remarkable similarity of Rogerian theory as it later developed to the philosophy of progressive education to which Rogers was exposed in his twenties.[20] The far-reaching parallels between progressive education and client-centered therapy extend to the very definition of man. It is as if the concept of man formed in Rogers as a result of his contact with the fathers of progressive education was the concept which he "progressively" developed in his own theories of therapy. Sollod makes the insightful observation that the close relationship between progressive education and Rogers' work can be demonstrated with excerpts from Kilpatrick's writings in which one need only substitute the term "client" for "student" or "child," "therapy" for "education," and "therapist" for "teacher," to transform a quotation from Kilpatrick into a statement of Rogerian theory. The substitutions are italicized in the following Kilpatrick statements:

> I should like to think of *therapy* as the process of continually remaking experience in such a way as to give it continually a fuller and richer content and to give the *client* ever-increasing control over the process.
>
> You value *therapy* as it remakes life? Yes, as it remakes life here and now, I mean the *client's* life here and now. I am accordingly not so·sure as to our old formal *therapies*, whether they best remake life. I fear they too often postpone remaking.
>
> We saw that growth and *therapy* were practically two ways of saying the same thing. This led to the redefining of *therapy* ... as a process of continuous growth.[21]

Finally, Kilpatrick states a typically client-centered principle in these words: "Whether any piece of learning [read: *growth*] is intrinsic or not depends upon the pupil [*client*] and his need of such learning [*growth*], not upon the teacher [*therapist*]."[22] Kilpatrick does, however, give somewhat more emphasis to the teacher as a source of authority than Rogers gives the therapist. Still, the import of Kilpatrick's teachings is to encourage a trust in the free growth and learning of the student, much the same way that Rogers, afterwards, was to advocate a trust in the client.

Years later, Rogers made the circle complete by turning his interest to educational process and reform, basing this on his experience as a psychologist.[23] Unquestionably, Rogers' ideas are ones which Kilpatrick and Dewey would have smiled upon. Rogers himself acknowledges this link as follows:

> In one sense, our experience is a rediscovery of effective principles which have been stated by Dewey, Kilpatrick, and many others, and a rediscovery of effective practices which have certainly been discovered over and over again by competent teachers. Yet the fact that others have come to somewhat similar conclusions, not only in the recent years but in the more distant past, takes away nothing from the vividness of our own experience of discovery as we have tried to implement our therapeutic viewpoint in the field of education.[24]

In summary, the case of Rogers demonstrates the close and in many ways derivative connection between selfist psychology and the progressive philosophy advanced by Dewey which still dominates much of America's educational system.

We have briefly noted in the preceding chapters that religious themes and language often surface in selfist theory. Let us look now at some of these prominent indicators of the religious aspect of Rogers' psychology. Recall such a statement as: "I shall assume that the client experiences himself as being fully received." This being fully received by the priest-therapist takes the place of being so accepted by God. But Rogers leaves undeveloped the important ways in which it is impossible for any human being ever to fully or absolutely *receive* another.

Again, Rogers' key concept of "unconditional self-regard" is simply a transformation of the devout believer's conviction of God's unconditional love for him and the command that he attempt unconditional love of God in return, into a full-fledged self-devotion. Rogers argues that this unconditional self-regard occurs when the client "perceives himself in such a way that no self-experience can be discriminated as more or less worthy of positive regard than any other."[25] Such a statement is completely at odds with the Christian doctrine of sin (indeed it comports badly even with the common human notion of moral failure), and is still more critically in conflict with the doctrine of God's judgment. In a similar vein, Rogers advocates that the "individual, in effect, becomes his own significant social other" and *"experiences* himself as the *locus of evaluation."* [26]

The self-love advocated in Rogers' theory works itself out in the very process of client-centered therapy. This therapy technique consists in large part of reflecting back to the patient his own feelings, combined with the therapist's support but without any direct advice. In its extreme form, no longer advocated by Rogers, the therapy is limited entirely to paraphrases of the patients' feelings plus general comments of empathetic support. The key word for understanding this procedure is "reflection." The therapist is like a mirror, reflecting the patient's emotional states back to him.

In a most uncanny fashion, this reflective or client-centered technique recreates for the patient the conditions that long ago were powerfully described in the classical myth of Narcissus. Surrounded by the almost imperceptible therapist-manipulated mirror, the patient is forced into at least a short-term case of narcissism. After all, what else is there to fall in love with? For in spite of the idealistic goal which self-theory has of trying to develop an honest self-evaluation, the theoretical principles of Rogers, unrestrained by sensible limits and moral responsibility, allow, even encourage, the patient to slide into a self-gratifying narcissistic world.

There are no doubt some young people for whom the Rogerian self-therapy is a genuine constructive experience: for example, those reared by overly moralistic, overly critical, rigidly authoritarian parents. (I have been told that such families still exist — though I do not know any. I assume they must be close to extinction.) The great irony is that the post-1950 generation, which has so enthusiastically embraced anti-authoritarian selfism, has probably grown up with the least authoritarian parents in history.

A final religious dimension of Rogers' theory can be seen by reference to what might be called the "Protestant" nature of his thought. For example, Rogerian therapy places a strong emphasis on the ideal of each person working out his own destiny without the interference of others. Second, feeling and intuition are trusted as guides for this process: there is relatively little emphasis on reason, and tradition and history are evaluated negatively. Third, there is an emphasis on experiencing in the present, in line with the teachings of many Protestant religious writers. The typically non-authoritarian relationship between therapist and client is analogous to the relatively informal clergy-laity distinction among Protestants.

The "Protestant" character of client-centered therapy stands out even more sharply by contrast with the "rabbinic" or "Catholic" quality of psychoanalysis. Here the trust is placed in the trained reason of the therapist (i.e., priest or rabbi), and in his (Thomist or Talmudic) interpretation. The patient is not expected to find his own light and live according to it, but rather to orient his life to the light of reason, balanced by the experience incorporated in tradition as expressed through institutional authority. The temporal emphasis is on the past or on interpreting the present in view of the past.

This split between "Catholic" or "rabbinic" and "Protestant" schools of modern psychology has been nicely captured by Christopher Lasch. Lasch, too, claims that psychiatry has taken on many of the features of a popular religion, but his focus in the essay in question is primarily on psychiatrists as they function in the role of this new priesthood. He then interprets the current intense theoretical strife within psychology as an avatar of the old Protestant-Catholic conflict, erupting in the new secular faith. Broadly speaking, Lasch argues that the schism is between "Catholic" and "Protestant" conceptions of the priestly function. The "Protestants" have translated psychiatric theory into the vernacular, in order to make it more accessible to their congregations. They have introduced innovations in psychiatric ritual designed to diminish the magisterial authority of the psychiatrist: ". . . the therapist should confront the patient as an equal and seek personal growth himself, instead of using his authority to justify a pattern of retreat and defense against the new."[27]

The "Catholics," on the other hand, reject the concept of a psychiatric priesthood of all believers and oppose the proliferation of all these new superficial store-front psychotherapies: "By no means indifferent to the need for changes in ritual and dogma, they nonetheless wish to preserve the profession's monopoly of the means of spiritual enlightenment. Condemning the spread of 'do-it-yourself' therapy, they insist on the need for psychiatrists to mediate between the sacred texts and the public."[28] Lasch goes on to argue that although the psychiatric "church" still stands, it is preparing the way for fascist forms of behavioral control by presenting itself "as a religion that seeks to provide a universal cure for the miseries of existence."[29] He concludes that the two conflicting parties in the psychiatric profession have sacrificed Freud's honesty, intellectual rigor, and more restricted understanding of psychotherapy in their attempt to provide sweeping spiritual consolations.*

---

*Freud was quite aware of the religious character of Adlerian psychology, whence much of the psychology used in selfism derives. He made a sharp distinction between religion and psychoanalysis, and claimed that analysts "cannot guide patients in their synthesis; we can by analytic work only prepare them for it" and "We do not seek to bring him [the patient] relief by receiving him into the catholic, protestant or socialist community." Freud saw the Adlerians as "buffoons . . . publishing books about the meaning of life(!)." Freud also noted that "If you wish to expel religion from our European civilization you can only do it through another system of doctrines, and from the outset this would take over all the psychological characteristics of religion."[30]

Chapter Seven

Selfism and the Family

The Isolated Individual

From the previous chapters it is clear that the concepts and values of selfism are not conducive to the formation and maintenance of permanent personal relationships or to values like duty, patience, and self-sacrifice, which maintain commitment. There is every reason to believe that the spread of the selfist philosophy in society has contributed greatly to the destruction of families. It is certainly no accident that many case histories in selfist literature are people in conflict with their spouses or families over some self-defined goal. With monotonous regularity the selfist literature sides with those values that encourage divorce, breaking up, dissolution of marital or family ties. All of this is done in the name of growth, autonomy, and "continuing the flux."

I shall argue here that the social destructiveness of much of today's psychotherapy can be attributed to characteristics of the therapy process itself, although psychologists assume that it is social or personality characteristics that are to blame when a client's marriage ends in divorce, for example. The problem begins with psychotherapy's neurotic preoccupation with the individual patient. This is reflected in the absence during most therapy of representation for the children, spouse, parents, and the like. Therapists tend to identify strongly with their patients, much as in the traditional relationship of lawyers and clients. Yet there is no analogy to the fact that in the legal relationship all the major interested parties have their day in court — at least some opportunity to state their side.*

Over-identification with and excessive trust in patients has plagued psychotherapy from the very start. One of the most famous examples is Freud's early belief that his patients' descriptions of having been sexually abused in childhood were in fact true. To his surprise he learned, by way of outside information, that such reports were usually false. The experienced therapist who knows the patient's background and is possibly even acquainted with some other members of the family can usually correct for such distortions, especially if a transference relationship develops (in other words, if the patient begins to relate to the therapist as though to a father or mother). Analyzing transference reveals how the patient is distorting interpersonal relationships, thus allowing the therapist to take these distortions into account. By contrast, in short-term, client-centered therapy, where the two parties are typically complete strangers, where the therapy is client-directed and rarely challenges the client's interpretation of the facts, where total trust is required by theoretical dogma, and where transference can hardly develop, little impediment exists to accepting uncritically the patient's account of things.

That these pressures in therapy tend to side with anti-family values would seem to be compounded further by the high proportion of psychotherapists who are themselves

---

*It is reasonable to suggest that psychotherapists should be liable for their contribution to any marital breakdown which results in great emotional pain for the other partner, since this is, in effect, a form of alienation of affection. The suffering of children caused by divorce is often very great; and in their case the possibility of justifiable legal suit seems especially clear. Since there are now many inexperienced, poorly trained therapists, especially those influenced by the popular selfists, this issue of psychological malpractice is probably quite real. No doubt most experienced therapists do not rashly encourage the break-up of marriages, but even the best of them frequently place much more value on their judgment of the patient's well-being than on that of members of the family. Social or religious values of the family usually rank very low, even with experienced therapists.

divorced, or alienated from their family and traditional religions. Such therapists have a normal human desire for social confirmation of their own life-pattern and thus may be the more inclined to encourage such a pattern in others.

Parents As the Source of Our Troubles

The anti-family effects of selfism are compounded by the overwhelming theoretical bias against parents in various schools of psychotherapy. This bias has existed from the beginning with Freud's postulate of the Oedipus Complex: that an intense hatred between father and son, first emerging in the child around the age of four, is the primary and universal experience in the formation of all male personality. What the father has done to merit this hatred is not especially clear. Apparently his crimes are to be married to the child's mother and to be big. Oedipal hostility can be neutralized through various means, for example, fear; but for many it is assumed to remain active throughout life, and it is always considered capable of reactivation. There is absolutely no corresponding emphasis on love of the father in Freudian or in selfist therapy — although the evidence of such love is certainly commonplace.

More recently, the theoretical preoccupation has shifted to the mother, who is now under a veritable conceptual barrage for being (take your choice) dominating, castrating, controlling, manipulative, seductive, emotionally dependent. The modern mother can't win either. In the case of both parents, it is high time that these "explanations" be called by their real name — a new variety of the old prejudice known as "scapegoating." When will psychological theory be honest and large enough to allow us all the dignity of accepting that the fault is not in our parents — any more than it is in our stars — but in ourselves.[1]

The ghost of the Oedipus Complex and of the bad mother can still be found in Transactional Analysis, where father and mother get collapsed into the unisex ego state called "Parent." In *I'm OK — You're OK*, for example, there is no doubt that the Parent, in spite of some good characteristics, is seen as the major cause of our troubles. The child is described as vulnerable, but otherwise as happy and good. For example:

> . . . Emerson said we "must know how to estimate a sour look." The Child does not know how to do this. A sour look turned in his direction can only produce feelings that add to his reservoir of negative data about himself. *It's my fault. Again. Always is. Ever will be. World without end.*
>
> During this time of helplessness there are an infinite number of total and uncompromising demands on the Child. On the other hand, he has the urges (genetic recordings) to empty his bowels ad lib., to explore, to know, to crush and to bang, to express feelings, and to experience all of the pleasant sensations associated with movement and discovery. On the other hand, there is the constant demand from the environment, essentially the parents, that he give up these basic satisfactions for the reward of parental approval. This approval, which can disappear as fast as it appears, is an unfathomable mystery to the Child, who has not yet made any certain connection between cause and effect.
>
> The prominent by-product of the frustrating, civilizing process is negative feelings.
>
> There *is* a bright side, too! In the Child is also a vast store of positive data. In the Child reside creativity, curiosity, the desire to explore and know, the urges to touch and feel and experience, and the recordings of the glorious, pristine feelings of first discoveries. In the Child are recorded the countless, grand *a-ha* experiences, the firsts in the life of the small person, the first drinking from the garden hose, the first stroking of the soft kitten, the first sure hold on mother's nipple, the first time the lights go on in response to his flicking the switch. . . .[2]

This myth of the intrinsically good and happy child (recall Maslow's similar assumption), with negative influences all coming from the outside, is a form of sentimentality almost touching in its naïveté. In fact, parents and society provide a whole array of positive influences: love, food, music, playmates, dances, nursery school, games, travel, crafts, stories. Such events not only give the child great joy, but they are the common, positive, observable, sustaining activities of a normal child's daily life. Of these experiences there is *no* mention. Nor are the negative experiences which the child provides for himself — intrinsic to human nature from the start — taken into account. The one-year-old's first jealousy; the first hatred, expressed by striking at another child (activities which appear to be enjoyed as much by children as adults); the easy way children learn the concept "mine" and the difficulty they have in learning "yours"; children's extreme self-centeredness; their remarkable capacity to become totally demanding tyrants — all this is ignored.

The efforts that parents and teachers put into helping children to share, to play together, to cooperate, and so forth are tributes to the natural negative capacity of children and to the natural positive influence of parent and society. Transactional Analysis by contrast sees the child as a repository of predominately not-OK feelings caused by the parents. The negative experiences are likened to tape recorder tapes, which are constantly replayed later in life. To escape entrapment in this horrible parent-caused past, Harris introduces a third ego state, also unisex, called the Adult. The Adult begins its development as follows:

> The ten-month-old has found he is able to do something which grows from his own awareness and original thought. This self-actualization is the beginning of the Adult. . . . Adult data accumulates as a result of the child's ability to find out for himself what is different about life from the "taught concept" of life in his Parent and the "felt concept" of life in his Child.[3]

This self-actualization is described as a kind of marvelous computer process. The Adult is:

> . . . principally concerned with transforming stimuli into pieces of information, and processing and filing that information on the basis of previous experience.
>
> The Adult is a data-processing computer, which grinds out decisions after computing the information from three sources: the Parent, the Child, and the data which the Adult has gathered and is gathering.[4]

As one might expect, creativity has nothing to do with the

Parent but originates in the Child's natural curiosity and is developed by the information-processing Adult. The Child provides the "want to" and the Adult provides the "how to," the essential requirement for creativity being "computer time," which is provided by the Adult. It is interesting that curiosity is considered a completely positive motive; its fundamental connection with aggression is passed over.

In summary the basic plot of the Transactional Analysis morality play is that the poor, defenseless, but intrinsically happy, good, and creative Child, burdened by the mean old Parent, is saved from losing the "Game of Life" by a self-actualizing information-processing computer called the Adult.

However simple-minded this theme of hostility to the parent, it has prevailed for so long that it has become second nature for today's therapists and for patients as well. Over and over we hear and read variations on a parody of the words of the returning Prodigal in Jesus' parable: "Father, you have sinned and are no more worthy to be called my father." The position that healing therapy can and should be built on love, gratitude, respect, and nurturance toward parents is completely unrepresented in the selfist writings. Imagine a therapy that regularly strengthened a patient's family. Why not use therapy to rediscover what the members of a family have in common, to recall the forgotten truths the parents provided but the patient rejected, to remember the parents' attempts to help which were rebuffed by a peer-spoiled or self-spoiled child? Many young people today have committed more psychological atrocities against their loving but bewildered parents than vice-versa. Indeed, among upper-middle-class families it is time to recognize the psychologically "battered parent" as a familiar syndrome.

In contrast to selfist psychology, traditional Christianity and Judaism actively support the family and the community. For the Christian the family is the basic model for society. Father, mother, brother, and sister are common terms for Christians in both Catholic and Protestant communities. All Christians are brothers and sisters as members in the mystical body of Christ represented on earth by the mother church. Everywhere the social emphasis of the church is on integration and synthesis. Judaism's remarkably strong support for the family is also well known. Many have explained Jewish survival in terms of this reverence for family.

For Christianity, the family is a small-scale, living embodiment of much of its theology: God the Father, Christ the Son, Mary the Mother, all of us as the children of God are prominent biblical themes. May we not then view an ideology which systematically denigrates or attacks the family, by structural analogy, as a force attacking Christianity? Consider, too, the central holy day of Christmas, which is a joyous celebration of motherhood and birth. May we not see that a psychologist advising abortion is acting in hostility against the deep structure of beliefs and meaning celebrated in the Christmas story? Recall that the young Mary was pregnant under circumstances that today routinely terminate in abortion. In the important theological context of Christmas the killing of an unborn child is a symbolic killing of the Christ child.

In the last decade the West in particular has become increasingly aware of how modern economic and technological systems pollute by treating part of the environment as separate from the rest. The analytic attitude (analysis means breaking into parts) which dominates contemporary science and technology soon destroys the pattern and integrity of the surrounding environment. Our argument is that in an analogous fashion modern psychology has created widespread "social pollution" by its analytical (and also reductionist) emphasis on the isolated individual and its relentless hostility to social bonds as expressed in tradition, community structures, and the family. It is no accident that it was modern industrial society which first reduced the extended family to the nuclear family, then reduced the nuclear family to the increasingly common subnuclear family of one parent, and now works toward the parentless family where the child is raised by government program.

Of course, the conventional wisdom for some years has been that the family has failed — hence the growing number of people seeking psychotherapy. But what is failing is not the family; what is failing is *modernism* with its analytic emphasis on the independent, mobile individual, caught up in narcissistic goals. This uncontrolled individualist search for personal gratification is as destructive of social ecology as the uncontrolled quest of economic satisfaction has been for our biological ecology. The answer to the meaningless lives of today's young people is to reduce the number of children being reared in shattered or non-caring families. It is not likely that this can happen unless there is a change in widely accepted beliefs about the value and importance of the family and about social bonds in general.*

One happy sign is that recent approaches to psycho-therapy have begun to concern themselves with what is called family therapy.[5] This, ultimately, requires a theory of the desirable or ideal family and certainly raises religious and ethical questions. Yet, the concern with the family is a concern with social integration and a refreshing move away from the extremely self-centered therapies that have turned so many souls into narcissistic social atoms.

---

*A symptom of America's need for family and community is the recent popularity of television shows portraying large successful families, e.g. the Waltons, Upstairs-Downstairs; the films about families facing challenging natural environments; also the interest in family history, e.g. Roots.

Chapter Eight

A Christian Critique

Selfism As Idolatry

It should be obvious — though it has apparently not been so to many — that the relentless and single-minded search for and glorification of the self is at direct cross-purposes with the Christian injunction to *lose* the self. Certainly Jesus Christ neither lived nor advocated a life that would qualify by today's standards as "self-actualized." For the Christian the self is the problem, not the potential paradise. Understanding this problem involves an awareness of sin, especially of the sin of pride; correcting this condition requires the practice of such un-self-actualized states as contrition and penitence, humility, obedience, and trust in God.

Some comments from Paul Ramsey's *Basic Christian Ethics* are appropriate.

> The first assertion Christian ethics makes about man is that he was created for personal existence within the image of God, and that Jesus Christ most perfectly reveals this image. The second assertion is that man is sinful. So fundamental is this doctrine in Christian thought that it cannot be overlooked. Indeed, many theologians regard it as basic equally with the first for any full understanding of man in the light of God. This has been the view not only of the more "pessimistic" thinkers; it was the view also of John Wesley, whose emphasis upon "going on to perfection" is well known.[1]

The Christian position is clear that sin is not exclusively or primarily something in society. It is something that all humans do, and do as a willed act, not merely as the consequence of outside influences on them. The locus of sin, therefore, is in the will of each of us. This central Christian doctrine has been under relentless attack for many years by almost all advocates of social science from traditional economics and sociology to Socialism and Communism. Ordinary Christians, undefended by their own theologians, have often succumbed to the position that evil lies only or primarily in society. As a consequence a central foundation of their doctrinal system has been undermined. A recent powerful and imaginative attack on the social science position comes from the Russian Christian Aleksandr Solzhenitsyn:

> Gradually it was disclosed to me that the line separating good and evil passes not through states, nor between classes, nor between political parties either — but right through every human heart. . . .
>
> Since then I have come to understand the truth of all the religions of the world: they struggle with the *evil inside a human being* (inside every human being). It is impossible to expel evil from the world in its entirety, but it is possible to constrict it within each person.
>
> And since that time I have come to understand the falsehood of all revolutions in history: they destroy only *those carriers* of evil contemporary with them (and also out of haste, to discriminate the carriers of good as well). And they then take to themselves as their heritage the actual evil itself, magnified still more.[2]

In spite of the anti-religious prejudice of modern psychology at least one prominent psychologist appreciates the psychological necessity of accepting sin. This is O. Hobart Mowrer, who has written as follows:

> For several decades we psychologists looked upon the whole matter of sin and moral accountability as a great incubus and acclaimed our liberation from it as epoch-making. But at length we have discovered that to be "free" in this sense, i.e., to have the excuse of being "sick" rather than sinful, is to court the danger of also becoming lost. This danger is, I believe, betokened by the widespread interest in Existentialism which we are presently witnessing. In becoming

amoral, ethically neutral, and "free," we have cut the very roots of our being; lost our deepest sense of self-hood and identity; and with neurotics themselves, find ourselves asking: "who *am* I?"[3]

The great benefit of the doctrine of sin is that it re-introduces responsibility for our own behavior, responsibility for changing as well as giving meaning to our condition. Mowrer describes these benefits from the acceptance of sin:

> Recovery (constructive change, redemption) is most assuredly attained, not by helping a person reject and rise above his sins, but by helping him *accept them.* This is the paradox which we have not at all understood and which is the very crux of the problem. Just so long as a person lives under the shadow of real, unacknowledged, and unexpiated guilt, he *cannot* (if he has any character at all) "accept himself"; and all *our* efforts to reassure and accept him will avail nothing. He will continue to hate himself and to suffer the inevitable consequences of self-hatred. But the moment he (with or without "assistance") begins to accept his guilt and sinfulness, the possibility of radical reformation opens up; and with this, the individual may legitimately, though not without pain and effort, pass from deep, pervasive self-rejection and self-torture to a new freedom, of self-respect and peace.[4]

The problems posed by humanistic selfism are not new to Christianity: indeed, they can be traced back to early conflicts with Stoicism and other sophisticated Graeco-Roman philosophical and ethical systems. To worship one's self (in self-realization) or to worship all humanity is, in Christian terms, simple idolatry operating from the usual motive of unconscious egotism. Unconscious or disguised self-love has long been recognized as the source of idolatry. Otto Baab, in his study of Old Testament theology, describes it thus:

> Idolatry is well understood in the Bible as differing from the pure worship of Israel's God in the fact of its personification and objectification of the human will in contrast with the superhuman transcendence of the true God. When an idol is worshipped, man is worshipping himself, his desires, his purposes and his will. . . . As a consequence of this type of idolatry man was outrageously guilty of giving himself the

status of God and of exalting his own will as of supreme worth.[5]

Such an analysis makes it clear that in religious terms selfist humanism is just another example of idolatrous narcissism.

After the establishment of Christianity the worship of the self continued as a many-faceted heresy. Elements of modern selfism are found in Gnosticism, in the medieval Brethren of the Free Spirit, and in many other sects.[6] The present form of selfism also contains strong Pelagian strands. Pelagius, a fourth-century theologian from Britain, opposed the doctrine of original sin and argued that man was capable of living a perfect and sinless life, thus downgrading the importance of God's grace.* Evans in a recent scholarly book points out that Pelagius' position was not as extreme as his critics have often portrayed it.[7] He remained a Christian theologian and even so vigorous an opponent of his as St. Augustine acknowledged him to be a "saintly man." But a strong element in his theology might, under the traditional and rather extreme interpretation of it, be viewed as akin to humanist selfism. So it has been accepted by Fromm, who cites Pelagius as an ally and representative of what he calls "humanistic" religion, in contrast to the "authoritarian" religion typified by Augustine.[8] Evans, however, notes that Fromm's categories of "humanistic" and "authoritarian" religion do not fit the theologies of either Pelagius or

---

*The humanist aspect of Pelagius' theology is sometimes said to be temperamentally natural to the English and by extension to Americans. There may be some small grain of truth here but the relative quiescence of Pelagianism in England for more than a thousand years after his death raises questions for such an interpretation. A more probable explanation would involve the unusual economic and social factors present in England in the latter fourth century, the formative time for Pelagius' thinking. The first was a preceding period of nearly two hundred years of increasing economic prosperity — roughly from the second to the end of the fourth century. This was the British-Roman period of country villas and baths. The second condition was the probable effect of the combined Roman and Christian culture — both powerful and civilizing imports to a previously pagan and rather primitive

Augustine. (This is just one example of how Fromm's bias in his writings concerning Christianity leads him to misread Christian theology and faith.)

Furthermore, with respect to the problem of authoritarianism, it should be noted that Christians from the beginning have been aware of the problems of excessive institutionalized authority and the dangers of bad faith which it can create. Over a two-thousand-year period the Christian response has been recurring spiritual revival and renewal. While there is a legitimate dichotomy between frozen, institutionalized or severely formalized religion and living, spiritual faith, authority *per se* operates in both types of religion. Today's bureaucratized, secularized, and highly humanized Protestantism provides an example of an overly intellectualized dead faith. Much of this Christianity has been drained of its vitality by an over-generalized psychology, of which an obvious example is the very humanist selfism Fromm espouses, which has become increasingly authoritative!

Like all popular heresy selfism has some positive and appealing properties. That you should look out for yourself is nice (and useful) to hear; that you should love and care for others is a familiar and great moral position. What is excluded is the spiritual life of prayer, meditation, and worship — the essential vertical dimension of Christianity, the relation to God. Selfism is an example of a horizontal heresy, with its emphasis only on the present, and on self-

---

Britain. Such a qualitatively new and superior culture combined with a substantial long-term increase in wealth could easily have created the belief in Britain and in some other parts of the Roman empire that a new era had dawned and the old laws of human nature and history no longer operated. Shortly after the death of Pelagius, about 431, Britain relapsed into wars, social breakdown, and barbarism — all of which may have provided more effective anti-Pelagian "arguments" than those of St. Augustine or St. Jerome. There is in this example an obvious historical similarity to America's two hundred years of greatly increasing wealth combined with the belief that science has ushered in a new condition of progress in which the old understanding of human nature and its limits is no longer relevant.

centered ethics. At its very best (which is not often), it is Christianity without the first commandment.

Christian Love and Selfist Love

Christianity and selfism differ not just over the self and self-love but about the very nature of love. To begin reflection on the Christian conception of love, recall that Christ summarized the whole law in two commands to love: "Thou shalt love the Lord thy God with all thy heart, with all thy soul and with all thy strength" and "Thou shalt love thy neighbor as thyself." The love of God is first. It is primary, and love of neighbor stems from it. Love in these two forms is at the very center of the Christian faith. Note, too, that there is no direct command to love the self — an adequate degree of self-love being assumed as natural.

This Christian theory of love has been expressed for nearly two thousand years in what is now an enormous tradition. It shines forth in the life and death of Jesus as recorded in the four gospels; it is disclosed in the writings of St. Paul, St. Augustine, St. Bernard, Martin Luther, Tolstoy, C. S. Lewis and many, many more; it is given contemporary application in a wide variety of personal and institutional practices. Christian love has been shown in the early Christian communities, in the age-old and still lively monastic tradition, in the expressions of medieval and Eastern Orthodox mysticism, in the emotional caring shown by pietist groups, in Christian hospitals, missions, and the Salvation Army. The lives of St. Francis in thirteenth-century Europe and Mother Theresa in twentieth-century Calcutta, of the host of saints and of countless other good quiet Christians are such remarkable and historically unique examples of the expression of love that it should be obvious that their faith had something to do with it. It is by turns flabbergasting and disturbing that nowhere in the selfist writings about love is this large body of Christian theory and practice ever discussed.

Fromm in his well-known book *The Art of Loving* presents what he describes as "The Theory of Love." In the discussion of love of God he follows the Feuerbachian approach by assuming that "the understanding of the concept of God must . . . start with an analysis of the character structure of the person who worships God."[9] Although he is less blatantly hostile to Christianity here than in his earlier work *The Dogma of Christ,* he does conclude, by various social and vaguely historical arguments, that the God professed by Christian theology is an illusion. His discussion of love does include some citations from the Christian mystic Meister Eckhart which imply that man is God. But these quotations are certainly not Christian and seriously misrepresent Meister Eckhart's theology. Eckhart's view of self-love is quite explicit: he calls it "the root and cause of all evil, depriving us of all goodness and perfection. Therefore, if the soul is to know God it must forget and lose itself; so long as it mirrors its own image it does not see or know God."[10] There is no word about keeping the self's integrity, using the self to define what is good, or any other of the familiar selfist themes. Fromm, in addition to misrepresenting Eckhart, completely neglects the major body of Christian writing on love.

Similarly, Maslow, in his major work *Motivation and Personality,* primarily discusses love between the sexes; and he has no Christian references. In some of his later writings, however, he does take seriously the mystic experience.[11] But Maslow's writings contain no treatment of Christian mysticism, much less any discussion of Christian love.

Carl Rogers in his best-known contribution to personality theory and psychotherapy, *On Becoming a Person,* has no treatment of love at all! Nor is love discussed in Rogers' book on encounter groups; and even his *Becoming Partners* has no theory of love — its emphasis is on sexual compatibility, changing roles and relationships, learning to trust the self and others, and the like. Needless to say there is no recognition or acknowledgment of the Christian theory of love.

As was pointed out above, it is essential in discussing Christian love to emphasize love of God — above all to emphasize that the love of God is for a Christian not primarily an intellectual dogma but an empirical fact, an overwhelming experiential reality. It is from this experienced reality that theology begins. In the final analysis all Christian theology is a theory of love, of divine love. Those unfamiliar with or dubious about such a spiritual state can translate "the love of God" into such terms as contemplation, meditation, mystic experience. This translation is *not* adequate for Christian theology, but will suffice for the present analysis.

The Christian theoretical claim is that love of God or Christ not only justifies the love of others, but also greatly facilitates it. St. Bernard's four-stage hierarchical model of the love of God is a famous twelfth-century conceptualization of the Christian's relation to the first commandment and the resulting consequences for the love of others. A brief summary of his position (from his *The Love of God —De Diligendo Deo*) exemplifies the kind of literature the selfists overlook. St. Bernard begins by saying that the reason the wise man loves God is because God *is* God, but for others amplification is needed. The first degree of love is "love of the self for self," which he assumes to be natural and good, unless it runs to excess when at this stage it should be controlled by the command to love one's neighbor as oneself. The second degree is "love of God for what he gives." For the Christian the initial reason for loving God is that God loves him, that God has loved first. This love, expressed in the creation of the world, reaches sublime expression in the New Testament, "For God so loved the world that he gave his only Son, that whoever believes in him should not perish but have eternal life" (John 3:16). Thus, this degree is love of God for his many blessings, including solace found in times of trouble. It is through this love that the Christian first learns his limitations and weaknesses.

The third stage is "love of God for what he is." In this stage God is loved purely for himself, because we "know how gracious the Lord is." In this degree the Christian finds "no difficulty in obeying the command to love our neighbor. The man who loves like this loves truly; and in so doing he loves the things of God. He loves purely and without self-interest."[12] This occurs, in part, "because he freely gives who freely has received." Finally, Bernard describes the fourth degree, which is difficult and rare: "A mountain is this fourth degree of love, God's own 'high hill,' a mountain strong, fertile, and rich. . . . Happy is he, and holy too, to whom it has been given, here in this mortal life rarely or even once, for one brief moment only, to taste this kind of love! . . . it is the bliss of heaven." This bliss can come about if we aim at conforming ourselves perfectly to the Creator and "living according to his will."[13]

The aligning of one's will with that of God in this fourth stage is described by St. Bernard:

> as molten, white hot iron is so like the fire, it seems to have renounced its natural form; as air when flooded with the sun's pure light is so transformed as to appear not lit so much as very light itself; so, with the saints, their human love will ineffably be melted out of them and all poured over, so to speak, into the will of God.[14]

This final degree allows the love of one's self "for God's sake," that is, loving oneself as God loves every person.

The tradition of Christian mysticism is rich in its descriptions of problems met on the path to the highest stage; and there is no insistence that only by reaching this stage can one be a Christian, though at least degree two is expected. Several hundred years later Martin Luther was to describe Christian love in a less mystical, more Christ-centered, but equally moving manner. Faith, Luther wrote, "snatches us away from ourselves and puts us outside ourselves." Again, "everyone should 'put on' his neighbor, and so conduct himself toward him as if he himself were in the other's place. A Christian man lives not in himself but in Christ and his neighbor. . . . He lives in Christ through faith, in his neighbor through love."[15]

The logic of such Christ-centered love is lucidly outlined in the following passage from Sir John Seely's *Ecce Homo* (1865).

> Now as the difficulty of discovering what is right arises commonly from the prevalence of self-interest in our minds, and as we commonly behave rightly to anyone for whom we feel

affection or sympathy, Christ considered that he who could feel sympathy for all would behave rightly to all. But how to give to the meagre and narrow hearts of men such enlargement? How to make them capable of a universal sympathy? Christ believed it possible to bind men to their kind, but on one condition — that they were first bound fast to Himself. He stood forth as the representative of men, He identified Himself with the cause and with the interests of all human beings, He was destined, as He began before long obscurely to intimate, to lay down His life for them. Few of us sympathize originally and directly with this devotion; few of us can perceive in human nature itself any merit sufficient to evoke it. But it is not so hard to love and venerate Him who felt it. So vast a passion of love, a devotion so comprehensive, has not elsewhere been in any degree approached, save by some of His imitators. And as love provokes love, many have found it possible to conceive for Christ an attachment the closeness of which no words can describe, a veneration so possessing and absorbing the man within them, that they have said: "I live no more, but Christ lives in me." Now such a feeling carries with it of necessity the feeling of love for all human beings. It matters no longer what quality men may exhibit; amiable or unamiable, as the brothers of Christ, as belonging to His sacred and consecrated kind, as objects of His love in life and death, they must be dear to all to whom He is dear.[16]

In each case, the love of God and Christ is said to increase a person's love of others and of all creation. The Christian form of love is not an abstract caring for humanity in general, of the sort that is often found in people who have little love for anyone in particular, nor is it a love for the common aspects of all humanity found in each person. It is a strong, overflowing love of each particular human being, warts and all. However poorly most Christians live up to this goal, it is abundantly clear that Christian love has a rich and articulate theory which has inspired and changed the lives of millions, and any serious psychological theory of love must take it into account.

The defender of selfism may retort that the highest and purest form of love advocated by such humanists as Fromm has nothing to do with selfishness in any of its expressions. There are, indeed, very positive-sounding descriptions of this kind of love in Fromm's writings. For instance, he states quite explicitly that humanist self-love is the opposite of selfishness and narcissism. He defines humanist self-love as union with the loved one while preserving one's own integrity; this love involves active concern and care for the other.[17] In spite of this admittedly inspiring conception of love the spread of self-theory psychology has resulted in a rapid dilution of the higher aspects of selfism and in more and more of the kinds of abuses we have described previously. The frequent collapse of higher selfist ideals may be attributed directly to many of the other, more fundamental concepts found in the selfist position. Selfist theory emphasizes the isolated conscious self as the sole judge of what the self should value and how it should act. Such an emphasis almost guarantees the breakdown of the higher ideals into a rationalization of selfishness permeated with narcissism. Hostility toward tradition and any other authority tends to have similar effects. It is no wonder that narcissism is the most rapidly increasing clinical syndrome and a lively theoretical issue in psychotherapy today.*

The individual Christian, at least if he is serious, has many guides to keep him away from extreme selfishness. First, there is the love of God, expressed in faith and in contemplative and meditative prayer. There is also the Christian's awareness of man's deep potential for sin and the need to be alert to the traps and delusions of the world. Further, there is the religious community — Christian friends,

---

*Heinz Kohut and Otto Kernberg are among those who have documented a dramatic increase in narcissistic problems. In part this is an increase in the amount of narcissistic attachment to the self but it also involves an increased instability in people's self-evaluations. For example, today's externally controlled evaluations often lead to intense self-love and self-esteem followed by self-hate and then a general mood of meaninglessness. The collapse of legitimate authority and meaning combined with the disintegration of family relationships contribute much to this problem, since internalized structures of meaning are necessary for stable self-evaluations. Such people are potentially very open to authoritarian social movements like est, the cult of Reverend Sun Myung Moon, and the like. We shall return to the subject of narcissism in Ch. 10.[18]

prayer groups, retreats, the supportive aid of the church and clergy. There is the emphasis on penance, on confession (especially in prayer), Christian doctrine, the creeds, the communion of saints. All these combine to help the practicing Christian not only keep from surrendering to the persistent desire to return to selfism but also arrive at higher levels of love and spiritual knowledge.

Creativity and the Creator

For the selfist creativity is conceived as personal growth through self-expression, and hence as an achievement. It is the way the individual self gains value, very often in comparison to others. In a sense wealth, intelligence, and integrity all take a back seat today to this truly middle-class value of "creativity." Most application forms for graduate and professional schools give prominence to it, and to be labeled creative has become the ultimate goal for millions.

For Christians the emphasis is very different: it is on developing one's abilities in the service of God and others, as shown in Christ's parable of the talents. C. S. Lewis describes the Christian's indifference or antipathy to preoccupation with creativity:

> Nothing could be more foreign to the tone of scripture than the language of those who describe a saint as a "moral genius" or a "spiritual genius." Thus insinuating that this virtue or spirituality is "creative" or "original." If I have read the New Testament aright, it leaves no room for "creativeness" even in a modified or metaphorical sense. Our whole destiny seems to lie in the opposite direction, . . . in acquiring a fragrance that is not our own but borrowed, in becoming clean mirrors filled with the image of a face that is not ours.[19]

Therefore a Christian artist or writer should never strive for creativity *per se* but instead should try to embody some reflection of eternal beauty and wisdom. Lewis notes that the Christian approach to literature, for example, groups itself with certain existing theories of literature as against others.

The Christian position

> would have affinities with the primitive or Homeric theory
> in which the poet is the mere pensioner of the Muse. It would
> have affinities with the Platonic doctrine of transcendent
> form partly imitable on earth; . . . it would be opposed to
> the theory of genius as, perhaps, generally understood; and
> above all it would be opposed to the idea that literature is
> self-expression.[20]

The Nature of Suffering

A final profound conflict between Christianity and selfism
centers around the meaning of suffering. The Christian
acknowledges evil — with its consequent pain and ultimately
death — as a fact of life. Through the Christian's losing
of his ordinary self in discipleship, in the imitation of Christ,
such suffering can serve as the experience out of which a
higher spiritual life is attained. This fundamental view is at
the very heart of Christianity, as represented by the passion
of the cross followed by the joy of Easter. All the great
religions accept the existence of sin, illusion, and death
and then provide a way to transform and transcend it. This
Way is always terribly difficult, but when successfully
traveled it is described in the highest terms. Most of us fear
the sacrifice and challenge which the true religious life
presents; as a result all over the world the genuine saint
or holy man is a hero.

In contrast selfist philosophy trivializes life by claiming
that suffering (and by implication even death) is without
intrinsic meaning. Suffering is seen as some sort of absurdity,
usually a man-made mistake which could have been avoided
by the use of knowledge to gain control of the environment.
The selfist position sounds optimistic and plausible particularly when advocated during materially prosperous times. But
it is a superficial view, which loses its convincing character
with wider experience of a kind that is now becoming
common. Millions who enthusiastically endorsed optimistic
selfism in the prime of life are now beginning to experience

the ancient lessons of physical decline, of loss, of sickness and death — lessons which puncture all superficial optimism about the continued happy growth of the wonderful self. Even institutions have begun to be haunted by the specters of age and death. And materialistic optimism is further undermined by the growing publicity given to such intractable problems as resource exhaustion, nuclear war, worldwide weather shifts, famines, chronic inflation, huge unrepayable debts, the worldwide retreat of democracy.

What does one tell a chronically over-ambitious man who learns at age forty that further advancement is over and that he has a serious, possibly fatal, illness? What does one tell a woman whose early career hopes have ended in a wearisome and dead-end bureaucratic job? What does one say to the older worker who has lost his job, whose skills are not wanted? What does one tell the woman who is desperately alone inside an aging body and with a history of failed relationships? Does one advise such people to become more autonomous and independent? Does one say "go actualize yourself in creative activity"? For people in those circumstances such advice is not just irrelevant, it is an insult. It is exactly such suffering, however, which is at the center of the meaning and hope of the religious life. By starting with an unsentimental realism about existence religion is able to provide an honest and ultimately optimistic understanding of the human condition. Christianity starts with suffering and ends with joy. Selfist-humanism starts with optimism but ends in pessimism. And its pessimism is doubly depressing, for in spite of its many religious characteristics, the selfist position is in the final analysis a kind of false or substitute religion based on denying the *meaning* in suffering and death, experiences from which it cannot protect us.

* * *

We may now summarize the critical points raised against selfism in the preceding chapters. The basic assumption of humanistic selfism — namely the complete goodness of man's nature (as opposed to the evil influence from society) — receives extremely strong criticism from a wide variety of scientists and support from remarkably few. The humanists' central concept of the conscious self is poorly defined, filled with contradictions and seriously inadequate as a description of our psychological nature and as a tool for serious psychotherapy. Self-theory psychology has not shown the systematic development of a traditional science, in which replicated findings and increasingly precise concepts lead one generation to build on the work of the other. Instead, self-theories have turned into popular and commercialized ideologies with concepts that, if anything, are even more vague and diffuse than those of forty years ago. The popularization of selfism is attributable in large part to the recent period of rapid economic growth in an already wealthy and secularized society, with a large and growing population of young people. Certainly it is difficult to imagine self-actualization as a popular concept except in a period of great wealth and leisure. The suitability of selfism for rationalizing a consumer mentality and as a justification for natural tendencies to narcissistic self-indulgence has further increased its popularity. In spite of the non-scientific character of humanistic selfism, it has frequently claimed to be or allowed itself to be taken as a science and, as a result of this misrepresentation, it has gained greatly in money, power, and prestige.

Historically selfism derives from an explicitly anti-Christian humanism and its hostility to Christianity is a logical expression of its very different assumptions about the nature of the self, of creativity, of the family, of love, and of suffering.

In short, humanistic selfism is not a science but a popular secular substitute religion, which has nourished and spread today's widespread cult of self-worship.

Chapter Nine

Christian Politics

The Problem for Psychology

Whether or not it understands the situation the profession of psychology finds itself in a seriously compromised position because of its advocacy of the humanist-selfist religion. An organizational symptom of this is the large Humanistic Psychology Division of the American Psychological Association (APA). The problem raised by the nonscientific character of humanistic psychology has already caused serious controversy within the discipline. Traditional psychological scientists are deeply concerned by what they see as the erosion of the legitimate standards of objectivity for any science. D. O. Hebb very effectively expressed this concern in his 1973 presidential address to the APA. He presented the claim that psychology is a biological science and that trying to make it humanistic results in something which is neither satisfactory science nor satisfactory humanism.[1] One honest option, urged by Hebb, is for psychology to purge itself of or shake off its religious elements and return to its original, more limited, but legitimate, scientific character.

The selfist response to such attacks is to attempt to redefine science so as to include their position. This ends up making the concept of science vague beyond any usefulness. More importantly, it allows the traditional religions to fall clearly within the definition of science! Needless to say, humanist psychologists have no desire to allow Christian, Jewish, or other religious doctrines to intrude into "their" psychology. They want to broaden the concept of science enough to allow their work to be categorized under such a socially, politically, and economically powerful rubric, but they do not want to allow traditional religions the advantages of the same ploy. It is exactly this intellectual misrepresentation which they have used so effectively in the advocacy of their secular faith.

One possible resolution of this dilemma is for professional and academic psychologists to accept the psychology of the traditional religions. In the past it has been common in American organizations of academic disciplines to accept the demands of all large groups that seem reasonably appropriate. But in this case much of psychology's pretense to being a science — at least in the traditional sense — would be undermined. And those experimental psychologists who interpret psychology as a biological science would surely be alienated. Important difficulties about funding psychological activities with tax receipts would also be raised.

What will happen in the politics of the psychological profession is hard to say, but serious, direct challenges to the *status quo* are certainly called for.

The Problem for Christianity

Although the enthusiasm for selfism has probably begun to wane already, a whole generation has been deeply influenced by it. Christianity, I fear, has greatly underestimated both its power and the prevalence of the institutionalization of its value system. Selfism is now the standard position of much of the government bureaucracy that deals with social problems. It is certainly the controlling system in the so-called "helping" professions — clinical psychology, counseling, and social work. Irving Kristol has aptly described the same situation as found in the education establishment:

> We have a kind of faith in the nature of people that we do not have in the botanical processes of nature itself — and I use the word "faith" in its full religious force. We really do believe that all human beings have a natural *telos* toward becoming flowers, not weeds or poison ivy, and that aggregates of human beings have a natural predisposition to arrange themselves

into gardens, not jungles or garbage heaps. This sublime and noble faith we may call the religion of liberal humanism. It is the dominant spiritual and intellectual orthodoxy in America today. Indeed, despite all our chatter about the separation of church and state, one can even say it is the official religion of American society today, as against which all other religions can be criticized as divisive and parochial.[2]

The reason for this dominance is clear. The government bureaucracy in general, and the "helping professions" in particular, must have an ethic by which to set goals and priorities and evaluate procedures. This ethic must be non-controversial yet inspiring if it is to be justified to the legislature and the electorate. Being "for people," and programs that "help you help yourself" are the most positive among the lowest common denominators available.

In frequent contacts with clinical psychologists, I have found selfism almost unanimous. When a Christian view is mentioned, they are amused as though being shown an antique. If the suggestion of Christian withdrawal from or revolt against selfist values is made, the reaction is one of anger or irritation. Psychologists today are indifferent to Christianity because they rarely hear it advocated in their professional environment; when it is brought to their attention the hostility is clear.

Fifty years ago the "helping professions" were of little consequence; today they are large and growing rapidly as the government expands its social services. The accompaniment of this growth by the self-theory ethic constitutes a powerful new challenge to the Christian faith. There is little reason to believe this secular religion will change over the years, since it is not some arbitrary choice based on a fad in the 1960s; it is a necessary part of the extension of government programs into every aspect of our lives. Many of these programs have made it harder and harder to be both a good Christian and a good American.

Let us look briefly at some of the particular policies currently expressing selfism through government programs. The newest area being staked out by these secular humanists is the "science" of thanatology, or Death and Dying (D&D),

as it is often called. New journals, government-sponsored research institutes, D & D study courses, and the like have turned death into the newest intellectual growth industry. Malachi Martin has characterized the main theory of death guiding this movement: "Death is transformed for everyone from a Doorway into a Wall."[3] That is, the religious concept of life after death is denied (more accurately ignored), and death is interpreted as the absolute end. The essentially religious nature of this problem is clear, and we see again government-sponsored programs and philosophy challenging and competing with Christianity.

Another particular example is the sex education programs now found in many of the nation's secondary schools. The initial ideological orientation of these programs is to exclude consideration of all attributes of sex except its biological ones, plus a few social consequences. But this denial of the moral, religious, and spiritual character of sexual relations is a prejudiced control of the ground rules for understanding sex, which guarantees what is in effect an *anti*-religious presentation to students as well as facilitating an aggressive desacralization of sex. Thus the secular value system is expanded. In terms of a legal analogy: the meaning and purpose of sex are on trial in a classroom, and the religious defense is not allowed to speak or even to be present. This denial of due process for the religious view within secular education is justified on the ground that a biological presentation is scientific and totally objective.

Complaining about the exclusion of the religious interpretation of sex cannot be dismissed as the expected position of a bunch of sexually repressed, moralistic, modern-day Puritans; instead, it is to be found among the most sensitive and sophisticated psychological thinkers. We quote again from Ernest Becker, who presents his own views as well as psychoanalyst Otto Rank's understanding of this problem:

> The questions about sex that the child asks are thus not — at a fundamental level — about sex at all. They are about the meaning of the body, the error of living with a body. When the parents give a straightforward biological answer to sexual questions, they do not answer the child's question at all.

He wants to know why he has a body, where it came from, and what it means for a selfconscious creature to be limited by it. He is asking about the ultimate mystery of life, not about the mechanics of sex. As Rank says, this explains why the adults suffer as much from the sexual problem as the child: the "biological solution of the problem of humanity is as ungratifying and inadequate for the adult as for the child."

Sex is a "disappointing answer to life's riddle," and if we pretend that it is an adequate one, we are lying both to ourselves and to our children. As Rank beautifully argues, in this sense "sex education" is a kind of wishful thinking, a rationalization, and a pretense: we try to make believe that if we give instruction in the mechanics of sex we are explaining the mystery of life. We might say that modern man tries to replace vital awe and wonder with a "How to do it" manual. We know why: if you cloak the mystery of creation in the easy steps of human manipulations you banish the terror of the death that is reserved for us as species-sexual animals. Rank goes so far as to conclude that the child is sensitive to this kind of lying. He refuses the "correct scientific explanation" of sexuality, and he refuses too the mandate to guilt-free sex enjoyment that it implies.[4]*

A detailed documentation of how tax money is used to support the selfist religion is beyond the scope of this book, but certainly the major way this happens is the massive tax support of education and, through education, many other activities such as the "helping professions." From Stanford and Harvard down to the local grade school the education of most Americans is permeated with selfist ideology. Prominent graduate schools turn out articulate proponents of these values, who readily find responsible positions in bureaucracies, big business, and the media, where their newly acquired

---

*A book such as *The Ideal Marriage: Its Physiology and Technique*, by T. H. Van de Velde, shows even in its very title the ideological character of the sex educationalists. This book is one of the bibles of sex education. First published in 1926, it has gone through many printings. The Random House edition, first published in 1941, had gone through 48 printings by 1970. The book's motto, found on the title page, is "Marriage is a science."

selfist religion continues to feed the secularization process. There should be no illusions about the attitudes which are prevalent in these institutions: Christianity is dismissed as a foolish, uncultured, bigoted remnant of pre-modern superstition. Pluralism is advocated as a disguise for secular humanist control of religions through the government/university/big business apparatus. Religion is seen as a form of local color, sometimes interesting, always assumed to be disappearing, never personally convincing to those who believe their consciousness has been raised above such limited earlier forms of thought.

That Christians are taxed to support large-scale programs which regularly teach anti-Christian theories is not just a serious case of intellectual misrepresentation, it has become a grave violation of the constitutional separation of church and state. Violation of this separation in the past typically has come from undue religious involvement in secular functions. It should come as no surprise that with the massive growth of government the situation is now reversed: the secular system which intrudes into all aspects of life has been using government-funded and controlled programs for propagating its own faith.

Conservative Christians too often intuitively recognize the nature of these conflicts without being able to articulate their position with much sophistication. Meanwhile, the liberal churches have often enthusiastically embraced selfism and humanistic psychology without regard to its hostility to Christian teaching. It seems high time to transcend both reactions with a post-modern, intellectually sound, counter-response regaining for the church the large, legitimate religious issues it has surrendered to secular ideologies like selfist psychology.

In addition to the development of an intellectual critique of secularism, a Christian political response is called for. I do not mean by this politics "as usual" — in the sense of ideological conflicts between left and right — for the usual ideologies of both capitalism and communism are essentially secular, and in their modern forms both are anti-Christian. Nor am I suggesting rallies, demonstrations, new political parties. What seems more to the point is the quiet but persistent, immediate but long-term withdrawal of support from the anti-Christian activities of the modern state, whether these emerge from the "left" (e.g., the Department of Health, Education, and Welfare), the "right" (e.g., the Central Intelligence Agency), or the "middle of the road" (e.g., the public school system).

The exact form this defense of the faith might take depends on particular circumstances. It does not fall within our intention here to develop a full-fledged theory of Christian political action in response to government-sponsored hostility to Christianity. But for one thing, more legal challenges by Christians to tax-supported secularization are called for. Public education — which is in effect *government* education, selfist in orientation and hostile to religion — is certainly one area of importance here. Serious consideration has to be given to the implications of keeping one's children in public schools; enrolling them in existing Christian schools or establishing such schools will often be a preferable course of action. Needless to say, everything possible must be done to prevent such alternative schools from becoming enclaves of affluent Christians, effectively closed to the poor because of high tuition rates. In many cases support can be withdrawn from government schools by voting against taxes or by encouraging voucher plans which give some kind of financial aid to religious schools, though, again, such action should not be undertaken without serious and informed considerations of its likely effect on other people, particularly the poor.

Christian alumni may wish to reflect on the directions taken by the colleges from which they graduated before responding to the usual pleas for financial contributions on the strength of recollections of an older atmosphere long since superseded. Why donate money where your gift will be used to undermine your faith? Investigate ways of giving money which will help support your religion rather than another selfist professor. Scholarship funds for Christian students may be an example of this. If a son or daughter is thinking of going to a secular school, ask the *administration* (not the local churches) what sort of environment is provided for the encouragement and development of students' spiritual lives. How does that compare with the environments provided to encourage and develop students' athletic, social, and sex lives — that is, to advance secularism?

There is considerable evidence of spontaneous Christian political action in some parts of the United States. The successful Amish challenge to laws making school attendance compulsory until age 16; opposition to textbooks seen as anti-Christian; legal action against the violation of religious freedom involved in being compelled to support a state school system which establishes the religion of secular humanism and discriminates against parents who choose non-state schools for their children based on their convictions; protests against the closing of small Christian schools for failure to comply fully with complex, massive, and vague standards for public education — all these embody a developing awareness of the need for Christian politics as a response to today's common anti-religious politics. In this struggle the more secularized Christian denominations are conspicuous by their absence. One problem with such Christians is that their lives are dominated by what is happening to and in the country, not to and in their faith. Others in this group seem to think that expressing religion forcibly against popular sentiment is somehow beneath the standards of social propriety to which they aspire.

A persistent Christian withdrawal from government-controlled schooling, combined with the continued growth of Christian education, could have profound effects. The secular establishment, however indifferent to or contemptuous of religion, does depend on broad public support. Withdrawal of such support combined with the development of alternative educational systems by Christians could greatly reduce the size and influence of the present secular system, particularly since it is already financially overextended, suffering from a well-deserved loss of public trust and self-confidence, and facing a fifteen- to twenty-year decline in the number of college-age youths.

Secular education has drained so much of the higher meaning out of higher education that students everywhere now see getting an education almost exclusively in terms of a job or a selfist career. Religious, spiritual, moral, and ethical ideals have all but disappeared, and with this disappearance wisdom and knowledge have degenerated into mere information, usually of a kind that rapidly becomes obsolete. No wonder parents and students are becoming more and more skeptical, especially at a cost of thousands of dollars a year. It is exactly this higher meaning, necessary for any education to be of intrinsic importance, which religion can supply.

One other expression of Christian politics is certainly called for — organized support for Christians all over the world who are being harassed, arrested, jailed, and martyred because of their faith. Thanks to Solzhenitsyn's writings the West has at least heard of the Soviet Union's systematic persecutions, though almost nothing has been done about it. Serious persecution of Christians has occurred in most Communist lands, with Albania being one of the worst. Nor are such persecutions confined to leftist governments: Christians have recently been harassed, arrested, and murdered because of their faith in Uganda, Zaire, South Korea, Chile, Argentina, the Philippines, Ecuador, Guatemala, and the Dominican Republic.[5] It is beginning to look as though there is a worldwide fundamental conflict between Christianity and the modern state — a conflict which has little to do with whether the state espouses a leftist or rightist political philosophy.

Chapter Ten

Beyond the Secular Self

The Bias in Being "Objective"

The assumption that the objective method of science is a fair and unbiased procedure for correctly understanding a phenomenon is widely accepted in modern society. I shall argue here, as a final major criticism of selfism, that, used in the study of human beings, this method is a profoundly prejudiced ideological tool, which leads inevitably to a particular theory of man.[1] Furthermore, the objective method is intimately connected with the growth of the modern self; specifically, I shall propose that the procedure of being objective is the fundamental psychological operation behind the growth of the self.

Before the case for the preceding claim is developed, it is necessary briefly to discuss the paradoxical relation of humanistic selfism to the objective method of science. A central argument of Rogers, May, and others is that the objective method is seriously inadequate for understanding human beings. The existentialists also asserted that psychology is intrinsically incapable of being a satisfactory natural science. Now in psychotherapy the objective method requires that the therapist interpret the patient through evidence such as scores on personality tests, and as exemplifying a category in some theory. That is, the therapist responds to the patient in terms of analytical and reasoning capacities. The selfists reject this as inadequate, and in contrast place great emphasis on the therapist's ability to identify with the patient, to empathize uncritically with him.

This humanist critique of the objective method represents a major argument about the limitations of science. In this respect, it is not only consistent with but very supportive of a religious interpretation of human nature, Christian or otherwise; here religion is clearly indebted to the humanists.

Unfortunately, in spite of the selfists' theoretical arguments about the psychotherapeutic relationship, for millions of people who have read and been influenced by them the actual consequences have been exactly the opposite. Self-theory has turned each person's self as it is experienced by him into more of an object than ever before. Never have so many people been so self-conscious, so aware of the self as something to be expressed, defended, and so forth. The self has become an object to itself. People talk about their self-image, their actualization, the way they used to talk about their social status, their car, or their stomach ulcers.

There is another unfavorable consequence of the selfist position. The emphasis on empathy and identification with others (for instance, the touching and feeling encouraged in encounter groups) has led to an over-reaction against reason and objectivity. One result has been a cultivation of the irrational in therapy, the rejection of reason, and a lowering of perfectly legitimate standards for training psycho-therapists.[2] From the Christian and Jewish points of view neither uncontrolled, mindless intuition nor too rigidly controlled, emotionless reason is acceptable.

With these points made we can begin the final critique of selfism.

Objectification is an intellectual act, central to all criticism, which takes a naive, unexamined experience and turns the source or cause of the experience into an object of study. That is, to *object*-ify, as the word implies, is to take an unself-conscious experience, in which the self and external cause are fused, and break it into a subject and object. The self is the subject, and the object is the outside cause of the *ex*-perience. What was a single experience is broken into two entities — the interior subject or self, and the object of study. This action creates a "distance" between subject (self) and object, which allows the object to be examined. The spatial analogy of distance is not defined precisely, but the point is that unself-conscious experience ("fusion") is like physical commingling of self and object, and objectification, or self-conscious knowledge, is like the self's stepping away from the object, hence creating a distance and angles of observation for the critical self.

The earliest or first state is the natural state of naïveté, which characterizes much of childhood and presumably the early historical periods of a society. The self-theorists' emphasis on empathy as a source of interpersonal knowledge represents a preoccupation on their part with a technique that to a limited extent recaptures the mentality of this first state. The second state is a period of increasing critical distancing — of denial of innocence — which gathers momentum as one new object after another is brought under study. The history of ideas is in many respects the history of the discovery of previously unexamined experiences which then serve as new objects of study.

The process of objectifying experience is fundamentally the process of treating events as *objects*. Early in life, when the child distinguishes between his own body and things external to it, objectification works well. But when human beings get treated more and more objectively, a variety of troubles sets in. The development of objective knowledge intrinsically involves a power relationship: the subject (self) has power over the object. In psychology, for instance, the development of *object*-ive knowledge about people requires experiments in which the experimenter has increasingly greater control (another name for power) over the person studied. The development of science is largely determined by the rate at which new techniques provide more precise control over the objects studied. To be treated as an object is to be under the power of the subject (self) who is studying you.

> The very terminology, *subject* and *object*, has an independent power quotient in grammar, where *subject* connotes activity and *object* passivity (note the verbal form *to subject!*), with the suggestion of the division of reality between animate and inanimate, agents and things, beholder and beheld.[3]

Since objective knowledge is based on the subject's controlling power over the object, it follows that any distinction between subject and object is inevitably a power distinction and therefore also a moral distinction. This well-known relationship is often expressed in the complaint, "You're treating me as an object." Women quite rightly complain when they are treated as sex objects, but the answer to this is surely not a mutual, competitive power struggle in which both women and men get treated as objects. Yet this is exactly what the scientifically "objective" approach encourages — while claiming to be an unbiased, morally neutral procedure for discovering truth.

It is this underlying bias which explains the ideological conflict over sex education. The entire biological presentation in sex education is a treatment of men, women, and sex as objects under the power of scientists, with whom the public implicitly identifies. The problem is not just that the religious view of sexual relations is excluded; it is that the morally loaded "objective" view is included — a view in which the basic bias is to treat people and sex as objects. The ultimate ploy of the advocates of sex education programs is to keep this bias out of the awareness of those involved by talking about the "objective scientific" nature of the biology of sex. Even when the opponents firmly sense the ideological nature of the problem they often founder when it comes to conscious articulation.

The Object's Revenge

The power gained by the self as it becomes the subject of more and more objects under its increasingly sophisticated control feeds self-growth. The process is experienced as actualization, as becoming autonomous, as becoming independent of the objects — the places, people, and customs — now located "outside," in the environment with which the self was first unself-consciously fused.

One outcome of this objective view so common today is well described by Hans Jonas:

Modern theory is about objects lower than man: even stars,

being common things, are lower than man. . . . (Even in human sciences, whose object *is* man,) their object too is "lower than man. . . ." For a scientific theory of him to be possible, man, including his habits of valuation, has to be taken as determined by causal laws, as an instance and part of nature. The scientist does take him so — but not himself while he assumes and exercises his freedom of inquiry and his openness to reason, evidence, and truth. Thus man-the-knower apprehends man-*qua*-lower-than-himself and in doing so achieves knowledge of man-*qua*-lower-than-man, since all scientific theory is of things lower than man-the-knower. It is on that condition that they can be subject to "theory," hence to control, hence to use. Then man-lower-than-man explained by the human sciences — man reified — can by the instructions of these sciences be controlled (even "engineered") and thus used. . . .[4]

Clearly the price of this growth is considerable. In time it becomes intolerable. If the subject is master and the object is slave, then in true Hegelian fashion there ultimately occurs what can only be described as the object's revenge. The object eventually conquers by reducing the subject to the object's categorical level. Again, Jonas:

And as the use of what is lower-than-man can only be for what is lower and not for what is higher in the user himself, the knower and user becomes in such use, if made all-inclusive, himself lower than man. . . . Inevitably the manipulator comes to see himself in the same light as those his theory has made manipulable; and in the self-inclusive solidarity with the general human lowliness amidst the splendor of human power his charity is but self-compassion and that tolerance that springs from self-contempt: we are all poor puppets and cannot help being what we are. . . .[5]

The master becomes defined by his slaves, the subject by its objects, the psychologist by his rats or pigeons or cats.*

---

*Just to teach psychology or to run experiments is to participate in the morality of the subject-object distinction. Indeed, perhaps the appeal of "objective" psychological theories is that they give power to the selves of those who understand and use them. This power is certainly the primary appeal of the popular "you-can-win-at-the-game-of-life" books discussed earlier.

The Dilemma of Existential Narcissism

Another and simultaneous revenge is a result of the terrible distance and consequent alienation from the objectified others. Naturally enough this distance creates an intense need for closeness, for love. When the distanced and controlled object is an automobile or a computer few problems result. When the process distances the self from spouse, parents, brothers and sisters, lovers — finally from almost everyone — the situation becomes desperate.

Some of the frightening, even pathetic responses to this developing situation have been poignantly described by Herbert Hendin in *The Age of Sensation*, a psychoanalytic exploration of several hundred college-age young people conducted in the late 1960s and early 1970s. Many of these were not patients but volunteers for the study. The students described were from Columbia and Barnard Colleges. They are not necessarily typical of the country, but they are representative of intelligent, upper-middle-class college youth from the country's major urban and suburban centers. Throughout the book there is not a single mention of religion as playing a part in the life of any of the students. As far as one can gather, the students and their families are living entirely without religious values. In this the students are characteristic of a generation reared almost entirely on pure selfist values and selfist psychology.

Hendin starts by defining this generation in terms of "its active pursuit of disengagement, detachment, fragmentation, and emotional numbness."

> The students I saw tried many escape routes. The main ones moved in two seemingly different directions: one toward numbness and limited, controlled experience; the other toward impulsive action and fragmented sensory stimulation. At times the same student alternated between one and the other. To perform, but not to feel, to acquire sensory experiences without emotional involvement were hopes which reflect the consuming wish not to know or acknowledge one's feelings.[6]

He goes on to describe their thoroughly selfist motives:

> This culture is marked by a self-interest and ego-centrism that

increasingly reduce all relations to the question: What am I getting out of it? . . . Society's fascination with self-aggrandizement makes many young people judge all relationships in terms of winning and losing points.

> For both sexes in this society, caring deeply for anyone is becoming synonymous with losing. Men seem to want to give women less and less, while women increasingly see demands men make as inherently demeaning and regard raising a child as only an unrelieved chore with no objective rewards. The scale of value against which both sexes now tend to measure everything is solitary gratification.[7]

What precisely do the young women want?

> When Thomas Pynchon wrote in *V.* about an eternal woman who had conquered her vulnerability to hate, love, and death by becoming a virtual automaton, he captured the dream of many young women. If marijuana was the drug of choice for men who sought in drugs reinforcement for withdrawal from parental demands for achievement and from competition, so amphetamines were the drug chosen by women who were determined to push themselves, despite their feelings, towards goals which had been set for them by others.[8]

Men are described in this way:

> Unleashed feeling, the explosion of the heart is so feared by most young men today that what they desire is not freedom but controls, checks to block any opening up of their passion. . . . They all saw feeling as destructive, saw passion as harmful to them and those involved with them. . . . If young women saw themselves as potential victims, young men knew and feared their potential for becoming victimizers.[9]

The response of both sexes was typically either robot-like control or sudden impulsive searches for sensation and experience which did not require involvement, most commonly in drugs and in casual sex — often homosexual.*

---

*Contemporary homosexual activism has been a major contributor to the tendency to treat men as sex objects. For example, the various rapidly growing male homosexual magazines commonly feature men as sex objects for other men; magazines such as *Playgirl* (a reverse mimic of *Playboy*), which are ostensibly for women, are reported to have a heavy homosexual readership.

In such an emotional climate romantic and idealistic love relationships are rare. One symptom of this, as Hendin notes, is that suicides over failed heterosexual love affairs are now uncommon, even though college-age suicide has increased. Today's students resist letting the opposite sex mean too much to them, and only homosexual men and women seem to interpret failed love relationships as significant enough to touch off a suicide attempt.

Another sexual indicator of a growing distance between men and women is increased male impotence:

> The growing body of clinical evidence indicating that impotence among young men is increasing points toward the frequency with which more and more men discover sex to be only another moment of withdrawal. The impotent students one sees now are not simply sexually passive. They are usually preoccupied with sex and actively engaged with women. But they are men whose fantasies and desires toward women are destructive and violent. Often they are men who consciously want to hurt women, who rarely connect their impotence with their hatred, but who know they regard women as enemies and sex as war.[10]

This pervasive male hostility toward women is of recent origin, and it arises from the experience of being treated as sex objects in relationships in which each person tries to objectify the other. Andy Warhol, in his chilling autobiography, comments on this and expresses an attitude which is now common and chic: "Brigitte Bardot was one of the first women to be really modern and treat men like love objects, buying them and discarding them. I like that."[11]*

In spite of the equality which men's new sex object status conveys, it is as evil for them as the corresponding

---

*Warhol's book is a disturbing description of the successful selfist who has mastered the problems of seeking sensation while holding on to an alienated self without commitments or deep relationships. Like Hendin's college students, Warhol alternates between kinky involvement in sensations and cool identification with machines. For example, he has had a long affair with his television set; he casually announces that he has been married to his tape recorder for years. (Hendin claims young people in their need to escape emotion actually "envy machines.") The

status for women has been for many years. The potential
social expression of this hatred of women could be very
serious. The possibility of a popular modern ascetic or
religious movement by men in which woman is portrayed as
a manipulating, degrading temptress is far from impossible.
To avoid such reactions it is necessary to stop treating sex
as an object, as an experience which men and women take
from each other.

Hendin's description of the family life of one of these
young women fits easily into a selfist model:

> She described her parents as "nice, pleasure-loving people"
> who are "sort of like camp counselors." She added that
> she "sort of liked" some of her counselors, even though she
> was miserable at camp. She said, "My parents aren't the sort
> who feel the family has to do something on a Sunday, so if
> they are together they get along fine because they are doing
> things that independently they want to do. If it happens that
> two of them want to do something at the same time, then
> it's OK. If they all had to go to the zoo together, they'd
> probably kill each other. They're better than families who feel
> they have to be together. My parents aren't the type who
> sacrifice themselves for their children. I don't think parents
> should."[12]

These highly selfist families are so captured by the
cultural values as no longer to provide a haven from the
outside world. Instead, the family is a center of self-
aggrandizement, exploitativeness, and titillation. Hendin
comments on the severe difficulties that arise when fathers
and sons regularly compete with each other in sports; each
is threatened by failure and guilty about success. The
increasing place of tennis, golf, and other competitive games
in middle-class family life can introduce an often destructive
competitiveness into the heart of family life, and certainly

---

book is an unorganized (spaced-out) presentation of the emptiness, shallowness, emotionless life of a culture "hero" for
many young Americans, who treats both himself and others as
objects. The various others in the book are indiscriminately
called "B"; he, being the subject, is called "A."

can provide "the game" as a model of a child's early inter-personal relationships.

Hendin often provides a clinical critique of selfism, one related to that presented here earlier:

> People out of touch with their feelings are strongly drawn to the idea that life consists of playing roles. Game playing (transactional analysis) goes even further in providing a model for how to deal with other people without even considering one's feelings toward them; . . . game playing is a parody of our concern with mastery and control.[13]

As a consequence of this emphasis:

> Society is fomenting depression in the trend toward the devaluation of children and the family. The increasing em-phasis on solitary gratification and immediate, tangible gain from all relationships only encourages an unwillingness in parents to give of themselves or tolerate the demands of small children. It is not surprising that the family emerges through the eyes of many students as a jail in which everyone is in solitary confinement, trapped within their own particular suffering.[14]

He concludes:

> The possibilities for the future depend on recognizing the present cataclysm for what it is, and on not leaving to chance that the forces for greater accord between the sexes will win out. How much contempt for love and tenderness is becoming institutionalized is only suggested by the new entertainments we are devising for young children. The frog, the toad, the troll who turns into a prince when kissed by a generous woman was the mainstay of the fairy tale, taught to little boys and girls for centuries. But in the modern Sesame Street version of the Beauty and the Beast when the princess kisses the beast she turns into one. Similarly when the prince comes to kiss Sleeping Beauty, the touch of her lips puts him to sleep too. We are teaching our children that intimacy brings out the worst in everyone, a theme rife in contemporary adult fiction.
>
> Young people in our culture are creating new ideal men and women who can resist each other's impact. The emotion-free, the controlled, the impenetrable, the invulnerable are praised as having characters geared for survival in the

modern emotional jungle. Students who had achieved maximal detachment from feeling are, in the new youth culture, admired as unshakable.[15]*

Hendin's brilliant descriptions portray exactly where so much of selfism ends: the self as subject frantically trying to gain control over others — the objects — in order to build its own self as subject. As more and more people have their "consciousness raised" — that is, as they are "liberated" from objecthood and take on the role of subjects — the competition becomes fierce. Life has become a game where there are only two states: winning and losing; sadist and masochist. Furthermore the new role of subject carries with it the almost unbearable memory of having been an exploited object in the past. This, plus the threat that the same thing might possibly happen in the future, raises to a high pitch the need to be the dominant subject. Intimate personal relationships become extremely dangerous. If you show weakness, such as a need for love, you get slaughtered; if you withdraw to a machine-like, emotion-free competence and develop complete identification with career you are isolated and starved for intimacy and love. Perhaps there is some relief in temporarily losing the self in sexual or other sensations and afterwards counting each new experience as a score for the self, but a lonely deathlike living is inescapable.

This painful double-bind leaves love of the self as the diabolically "safe" alternative. The trap cannot be avoided because it follows the fundamental logic of self-actualization, with its aim of developing the existential, autonomous self. Therefore, this syndrome might be called *existential narcissism*. There are other kinds of narcissism which result from neurotic experiences like an unstable or overindulgent childhood, but existential narcissism follows from a modern approach to living often chosen in adult life. Its end is the psychological death (in some cases the physical death as well)

---

*The many popular television heroes and heroines who are really machines or computers, e.g., the Bionic Man and Bionic Woman, can be viewed as expressions of this ideal.

of the self. Death may come from greater and greater devotion to sensation (sex, violence, or drugs) or from retreat into the isolated, machine-like world of the careerist ego — cold, calculating, often fueled by amphetamines. In either case there is an ever-tightening, self-inflicted solitary confinement based on continually repressing the need for love. One other out is obviously suicide. It is not too much to suggest that the 250% increase in the suicide rate for college youth over the last twenty years is a symptom of the spread of the existential selfist ideology.

Whatever the method of death, there is no escape from the conclusion that the modern self is intrinsically self-destructive.

Escape from the Self

Stage 1: The Naive Self or the Self As Object. As stated above, at first the self and object are fused in the naive unself-conscious experience commonly found in children. This stage generally ends because the principle of objectification is intrinsic to man and develops naturally with maturity as one compares and reflects on wider and wider domains of experience. The very young child first learns to distinguish the physical boundaries between self and the objects and people in his surrounding world. The Rogerian and Frommian emphasis on empathy and identification with the client or loved one are conscious strategies for recapturing the Stage 1 kind of knowledge. This is a legitimate, but limited, technique. Its great danger is that it easily degenerates into the search for sensations, such as drugs, sex, or violence, as part of a general over-reaction against reason.

Stage 2: The Selfist Self or the Self As Subject. The process of distinguishing the self from other entities — called objectification — as a person matures continues to expand into new types of experience until social customs, the values, beliefs, and personality characteristics of others, and finally the self are objectified. This activity of turning more and more experience into objectified knowledge creates power derived from the objects which the self controls. Using this power, the selfist self, or the self as the subject, continues to grow and expand. The willing decision to continually increase this power can be called the Faustian bargain — a "bondage of the will" at the center of the contemporary hubris. The price of this "bargain" is the large-scale alienation from objectified others and the meaningless, lonely nightmare as described by Hendin and seen in much of modern literature and film. Objective science is, of course, the major conscious cultural expression of this mode of thought. The conflict between Skinner and Rogers is really over their respective emphasis on Stage 2 or Stage 1 experience.

Stage 2 finally ends when even the self and the very principle of objectification are seen as objects. Once this happens, suspicion of the self as subject and suspicion of the process of being objective has begun. The quest for the authentic self is now seen as inauthentic. This suspicion is starting to spread throughout the West. It is manifest, however imperfectly, in the growing suspicion of science, technology, business, and government (i.e., suspicion of objectification and the systems based on it). It is also manifest in suspicion of the self, exemplified in the wide appeal of drugs and mystical experience, in which loss of the modern self occurs. These symptoms of the suspicion of a mentality basic to the West since the Renaissance are too varied and too natural an extension of modern thought to be dismissed as temporary aberrations. They signal that the waning of the modern age has begun.

Stage 3: The Transcendent Self or the Self As God's Object. The resolution of the preceding dilemma is religious, not psychological, and I shall describe it here in Christian terms. Very simply, the only way out is to lose the self, to let it go and once more willingly become an object again — not an object naively fused with the flow of life (except for brief moments this is no longer possible) nor an object to be controlled by other selves acting as subjects, but an object in the love and the service of God.

In order for this to happen one must let go of the selfist self and of its controlling will, bloated from constructing the interior apparatus of secular competence. This letting-go is no easy task, yet it is an essential one. With preparation of mind and will, transcendent awareness of God's love and will is possible by God's grace.

The movement to Stage 3 is never perfect or complete. It can occur in many ways. For some the change is sudden and intensely emotional — a conversion like that of St. Paul. For others it is the struggling development and maintenance of the true mystical life as represented by St. Bernard or St. Theresa. For others it is the slow, often sporadic development of a sense of being guided by divine Providence. In all of these cases reason plays a major role, indeed a necessary one, for feelings become distorted or vague or grow cold. In all of these cases prayer is essential. However short or long the period of transformation, it is aptly called a second birth.

The conditions that remove barriers and facilitate the movement to this stage provide a field of study for a Christian spiritual psychology (a field hardly in existence in any modern form). Although knowledge may be helpful in preparing for the transcendent stage, the major barrier is not lack of knowledge but the presence of the selfist will to power. It is precisely for this reason that the New Testament is so thoroughly characterized by motives and metaphors directly antithetical to the psychology of the independent, rebellious, autonomous, self-created self:

> Truly, I say to you, unless you turn and become like children, you will never enter the kingdom of heaven. Whoever humbles himself like this child, he is greatest in the kingdom of heaven (Matt. 18:3-4).

The same concern is expressed over and over when Christians are called the servants of God, and when the Lord is called our shepherd.

The third stage has important similarities to the first. It can be interpreted in part, in the familiar phrase of Paul Ricoeur, as a "second naïveté."*

There is little doubt that Stage 3 can be painfully difficult

---

*Ricoeur writes: "if we can no longer live the great symbolisms

to reach. Pulpits filled with talk about autonomous, self-actualized, self-determined, self-consciously, independently, creative, OK selves don't make the process any easier.

In conclusion, some personal remarks. The hardest ideas to deal with are those of the type just described, ideas that "threaten my ego." In spite of my rejection of self-theory, large parts of me remain which are still thoroughly indoctrinated with it. Particularly difficult are religious ideas like penitence, humility, accepting my dependence on God, praying for help. In my heart and in my mind I know these are good, true, and necessary for spiritual life. I know they are needed to curb pride and purge arrogance. But my yet luxuriant, overblown ego balks at and rejects being labeled "a miserable offender," wonders about the need for penitence, and occasionally bristles at metaphors referring to me as a sheep, child, or obedient servant. Equally foreign is the concept of judgment.

I know that many others who are not as ready as I to listen are turned away by these words at once. The justification for these concepts has been lost, and reeducation is desperately needed. We need updated orthodox theology. We need sermons on radical obedience, on the mysticism of submissive surrender of the will, on the beauty of dependency, on how to find humility. We all know it is hard for a rich man to get to heaven; I'm certain that it is even harder for a Ph.D. The problem for a Ph.D. — and I really mean to include doctors and lawyers and professionals of all types — is the problem of pride and will. Please, I would like to hear something that would improve my odds!

---

of the sacred in accordance with the original belief in them, we can, we modern men, aim at a second naïveté in and through criticism."[16] Criticism such as the present work only *aims* at the second naïveté; it is not the second naïveté itself. The kind of thinking characteristic of the third or transcendent stage is qualitatively different from modern criticism, which is still part of the Stage 2 mentality. True "second naïveté" thought is expressed most perfectly in Jesus Christ, less perfectly in the lives of the great spiritual leaders and saints. In a psychoanalytic framework Stage 1 thought can be understood as primary process thinking; Stage 2 thinking is secondary process thought — the reality-testing behind ego development. Taking this logic a step further, I would argue that there exists what should be called *tertiary thinking*, which qualitatively transcends secondary thinking.

Chapter Eleven

A New Christian Future?

The End of Modern Heroism

Disillusionment with modern society is familiar and wide-spread. As Ernest Becker and others have so clearly explained, the basic cause for this is the failure of secular heroic models to convince us of their intrinsic worth. We have consumed the heroic meaning in modernist life. The heroes are dead; even the anti-heroes have gone stale. The Great Revolutionary has dwindled to a part in political theater; the Communist hero is now seen as a functionary in the grim reality of the Gulag Archipelago; the socialist's ideal is a creeping bore; traditional politics has become a media-manipulated process of image control, in which show drives out substance, leaving the viewer with a residue of minor sentiments. The sports hero is a commercialized entertainer at best, a ruthless competitor driven by intense egotistical needs to dominate and make money at worst. Physical adventure and exploration have long since given way to the occasional self-conscious artificial creation of challenge such as rowing across the Atlantic or climbing up a mountain backwards. The heroic military ideal destroyed by the impersonal, frightening destructiveness of modern war has degenerated into the nostalgic reenactment of old battles in which a man's courage and daring once made a difference. The idea of a scientist as hero has eroded until what remains is the cold brilliance of a super administrator leading a team of technicians in a bureaucratic enterprise sponsored by some government, reported at a fancy international convention, and covered by the ever-present press; or, worse still, there is the growing role of the anti-hero scientist confronting us with the realities of nuclear power, genetic engineering, and more efficient mind control. The crisis is perhaps held at bay by millions of individuals attempting to find heroic meaning in the private neuroses of their personal careers. They fantasize tough-minded accomplishment surrounded by the soft rewards of various pleasures: stoical existentialism at work, epicurean consumerism at play. This double theme of a successful career combined with sensational, often decadent pleasure is standard with such contemporary women's magazines as *Cosmopolitan*. Their advertising and articles show the contemporary social value attached to the two responses of career and consumerism, the crippling strategies of so many of the young people described by Hendin in *The Age of Sensation*. Multinational corporations and government bureaucracies alike need hard-working professional types that are not tied down and are interchangeable across organizations; people who promptly spend their salaries to keep the consumer economy going.

But the pathetic inadequacy of pleasure as a route to higher meaning is obvious. One generation at most can pretend that such a response is "heroic" rebellion, but its degrading triviality cannot be long disguised. Again to quote from Becker:

> Hedonism is not heroism for most men. The pagans in the ancient world did not realize that and so lost out to the "despicable" creed of Judeo-Christianity. Modern men equally do not realize it, and so they sell their souls to consumer capitalism or consumer communism or replace their souls — as Rank said — with psychology. Psychotherapy is such a growing vogue today because people want to know why they are unhappy in hedonism and look for faults within themselves.[1]

The Coming Failure of Careerism

The failure of careerism is also coming. Indeed the first large-scale "career" crisis can be predicted with some certainty. Those in the middle of the post-war baby boom are now in their mid-twenties, the peak time for career expectations. This group represents a generational wave which by its very size has had and will continue to have a profound impact on American life. It is this group, reared on selfist psychology, which is especially committed to the career as the ultimate source of fulfilment. In part, these narrowly focused hopes are simply the result of the disappearance of other higher ideals. The universities, centers of selfist values, have also encouraged careerism for the pragmatic reason that they desperately need enrolments to stay in business.

We may sketch briefly the reasons why this group of people is headed for a career crisis of tragic intensity:

(1) Their expectations of success are unrealistically high, far higher than those of most generations.

(2) Economic growth in the United States has slowed considerably, and it is unlikely to come close to matching that of the last thirty years. Any major economic trouble in the next fifteen years would only make matters that much worse.

(3) Career dissatisfaction regularly strikes people in their late thirties or early forties. For the group we are talking about, this is only about ten years off.

(4) Many of today's popular careers, such as teaching, psychology, medicine, and law, are already overcrowded or becoming so. Future success in these fields will be severely limited.

(5) A very high proportion of today's career opportunities are in large organizations or bureaucracies. Such cumbersome systems invariably limit opportunities for advancement and destroy chances for effective, gratifying action.

(6) Many of today's young careerists will have no family to provide an alternative source of meaning and emotional support. The divorce and separation rate is very high among the generation of rising careerists; even ties with parents, aunts, uncles, brothers, and sisters are often weak.

(7) Many have chosen careers because it is the thing to do — not because of any deep interest in the activity involved.*

---

*Over the last ten years I have discussed psychology careers with

(8) Finally, and most important, careers are intrinsically too weak an ideal to carry the huge psychic burden they are now given. Even many in that small group who do succeed find success unsatisfying, even bleak and empty.

Together all these factors predict that this large wave is headed for a smash some time in the next decade.

The Emerging Opportunity

In the last three hundred years the intellectual orientation of the West has moved from a world-view derived from the distant material of the Newtonian universe to the much closer biological and social views of Darwin and Marx, to the psychological interpretation of life stemming from Freud prevalent today. Obviously physics has not lost its power to influence; yet over the centuries the dominant public orientation has somehow become increasingly less determined by physical science and more and more by the social sciences, especially psychology.

Within psychology itself over the last seventy-five years the center of emphasis has moved from the lower to the higher, from the unconscious and the Id, to the Ego and its defenses, to the self, then to the highest levels of the self, and recently to meditative and mystical states above the self. This historical tendency for the explanatory center of the mind to move to higher and higher levels bodes well for a spiritual interpretation of human reality.

The most exciting and positive parts of the self-theorists are their modest but genuine religious elements. For some of the self-theorists, mystic experience is considered natural and good. Maslow in his later writings, although backing away from genuine religious mysticism (he prefers to call it

---

at least two thousand different undergraduates — mostly psychology majors. In recent years, more and more of them choose careers for extrinsic reasons, for example, because of their parents, or of the general social pressure, or because of the need for some kind of goal after college. Today it is the well-socialized student who goes on to graduate training in some career; it is the unusual, imaginative, and interesting student who does not.

the "oceanic" feeling or peak experience), still cites such experiences as a positive characteristic of self-actualized people.[2] This sympathy toward both mysticism and the genuine valuing of love is a far cry from the hostile rejection of those states by the aggressively materialistic psychology of the nineteenth and early twentieth centuries. Although it has become common to refer to our era as post-Christian, the direction of change in science and psychology may equally suggest that the culture at large is at a new pre-Christian stage.

The search for transcendence of the self is now firmly begun. Browse in any bookstore, even those in small towns, and you will find a large section on psychology — mostly devoted to books on self-theory, sex, women's psychology, some Freud and a few other theorists. But close by there will usually also be a section devoted to *escape* from the self. Here are the books on Buddhism, the Tao, *I Ching*, Transcendental Meditation, altered states of consciousness, Yoga, and so on. We are all aware of the Eastern religious revival. The country is full of holy men — Sri Chinmoy, Maharishi, Yogi Gupta, Baba Ram Dass, and on and on. But where are the Christian holy ones? Where are the Christian mystical messengers to our pagan universities and suburbs?

Already there are many students, bored workers, young academics, professional people of all types searching for a life that is simple. Some want to live near the land, perhaps farm it, in a devoted and close community that will replace the family they have lost or never had. They want to withdraw from the technological society to a simple and enlightened life, but they don't want to drop out into an experimental commune where it all ends in a few years with petty bitterness and even deeper despair. They are prepared for a new heroism, and although they don't know it, they are ready for a genuine religious life. Some are even ready for a monastic life, although most have never known a monk or nun, or visited a monastery. They may reject at present the rule of celibacy, but even that rejection is waning. The preoccupation with sex may still be widespread, but many are becoming increasingly indifferent to it. Those on the leading edge of the baby boom are moving into their middle thirties where sex isn't what it used to be. And the emphasis on extreme kinds of sex, like sado-masochism and group sex, is probably a sign of the final stages of America's sex boom.

Here is how Becker perceptively states the situation:

> Today religionists wonder why youth has abandoned the churches, not wanting to realize that it is precisely because organized religion openly subscribes to a commercial-industrial hero system that is almost openly defunct; it so obviously denies reality, builds war machines against death, and banishes sacredness with bureaucratic dedication. Men are treated as things and the world is pulled down to their size. The churches subscribe to this empty heroics of possession, display, manipulation. I think that today Christianity is in trouble not because its myths are dead, but because it does not offer its ideal of heroic sainthood as an immediate personal one to be lived by believers. In a perverse way, the churches have turned their backs both on the miraculousness of creation *and* on the need to do something heroic in this world.[3]

In another ten years millions of people will be bored with the cult of the self and looking for a new life. The uncertainty is not the existence of this coming wave of returning prodigals, but whether their Father's house, the true faith, will still be there to welcome and celebrate their return.

Notes

About This Book

1. For a somewhat technical but extremely effective criticism of Skinner's philosophy of psychology see Karl Schick, *Skinner's Earlier and Later Behaviorism* (in press, 1977).

2. A good introduction is Charles T. Tart (ed.), *Transpersonal Psychologies* (New York: Harper, 1975).

Chapter One

1. See Heinz Hartmann, "Psychoanalysis and the Concept of Health," *International Journal of Psychoanalysis*, XX (1939), 308-321; Anna Freud, *The Ego and the Mechanisms of Defense* (London: Hogarth, 1942); Ernst Kris, "Ego Psychology and Interpretation in Psychoanalytic Therapy," *Psychoanalytic Quarterly*, XX (1951).

2. For example, R. D. Laing, *The Divided Self* (New York: Random House, 1969). A fine Christian critique of the Jungian self is in William A. Johnson's *The Search for Transcendence* (New York: Harper, 1974), pp. 140ff.

3. See Erich Fromm, *Escape from Freedom* (New York: Farrar and Rinehart, 1941); Erich Fromm, *The Dogma of Christ and Other Essays* (New York: Holt, Rinehart and Winston, 1955). Also relevant are *You Shall Be As Gods* (New York: Holt, Rinehart and Winston, 1966), and *The Sane Society* (New York: Rinehart, 1955).

4. Erich Fromm, *Man for Himself* (New York: Rinehart, 1947); quoted from the Fawcett Premier Book edition), pp. 13f. Italics in original.

5. *Ibid.*, p. 17.

6. *Ibid.*, p. 23. Italics in original.

7. *Ibid.*, p. 212.

8. *The Dogma of Christ*, p. 15.

9. Quoted in Calvin S. Hall and Gardner Lindzey, *Theories of Personality* (New York: Wiley, 1957), p. 476 — the source for other biographical information about Rogers, Fromm, and Maslow.

10. *On Becoming a Person* (Boston: Houghton Mifflin, 1961), pp. 37f. Italics added.

11. *Ibid.*, p. 130. Italics added.

12. *Ibid.*, p. 131.

13. *Ibid.*, pp. 135f. Italics in original.

14. *Ibid.*, pp. 139f. Italics in original.

15. *Ibid.*, p. 158.

16. Abraham Maslow, *Motivation and Personality* (New York: Harper, 2d ed., 1970), Ch. 11.

17. *Ibid.*, pp. 169f.

18. *Ibid.*, p. 152.

19. Rollo May, *Existence* (New York: Basic Books, 1958), p. 43.

20. *Ibid.*, p. 11.

21. *Ibid.*, p. 50.

22. *Ibid.*, p. 82; quoted from Carl Rogers, "Persons or Science? A Philosophical Question," *American Psychologist*, X (1955), 267-278.

23. Jean-Paul Sartre, *Being and Nothingness*, trans. by Hazel E. Barnes (New York: Philosophical Library, 1956), p. 561.

Chapter Two

1. Carl R. Rogers, *Carl Rogers on Encounter Groups* (New York: Harper & Row, 1970), pp. 7f.

2. Jut Meininger, *Success Through Transactional Analysis* (New York: Signet, 1973); now in 6th paperback printing. The quotation, which is representative of the text, is from the book's cover.

3. See Frederick S. Perls, *Gestalt Therapy Verbatim* (Lafayette, Calif.: Real People Press, 1969).

4. Robert J. Ringer, *Winning Through Intimidation* (New York: Funk and Wagnalls, 1974). See *New York Times Book Review*, Sept. 29, 1975, p. 17.

5. See Pat R. Marks, *est: Werner Erhard* (Chicago: Playboy Press, 1974). The information that follows was taken from various chapters in this book.

6. Carl Frederick, *est: Playing the Game the New Way* (New York: Dell, 1974). The quotations are from the Delta Paperback edition, 1976, pp. 171, 177, 168, 174, 190, 211f. Italics in original.

7. Carl Rogers, *On Being a Real Person*, p. 122.

8. Jean-Paul Sartre, *Existentialism* (New York: Philosophical Library, 1947), p. 58; see also *Words* (Greenwich, CT: Fawcett, 1964), pp. 156f.

9. John Money, "Recreational and Procreational Sex," *New York Times*, Sept. 13, 1975, p. 23.

10. Nena O'Neill and George O'Neill, *Open Marriage* (New York: Evans, 1972), pp. 253f. When the "open marriage" dissolves (as the O'Neills' did a couple of years after their book appeared), one resource available for the devotee of popularized self-theory is Mel Krantzler, *Creative Divorce: A New Opportunity for Personal Growth* (New York: Signet, 1973).

11. Caroline Gordon, *Beginner's Guide to Group Sex: Who Does What to Whom and How* (New York: Simon and Schuster, 1974), p. 156.

Chapter Three

1. Erich Fromm, *Psychoanalysis and Religion* (New Haven: Yale U.P., 1950), p. 21.

2. John Dewey, *A Common Faith* (New Haven: Yale U. P., 1934), p. 87. Italics added.

3. For a fine defense of the unchanging character of Christian doctrine, see C. S. Lewis, *God in the Dock* (Grand Rapids: Eerdmans, 1970), ch. 3.

4. Jeffrey Mehlman, "The 'Floating Signifier': from Levi-Strauss to Lacan," in *French Freud: Structural Studies in Psychoanalysis* (Yale French Studies, No. 48, 1972).

5. Konrad Lorenz, *On Aggression* (New York: Harcourt, Brace & World, 1966); Niko Tinbergen, "On War and Peace in Animals and Man," *Science,* CLX (1968), 1411-18.

6. René Dubos, "The humanizing of humans," *Saturday Review/World,* December 12, 1974, p. 76.

7. Ludwig von Bertalanffy, *Robots, Men and Minds* (New York: Braziller, 1967), Part 1, esp. p. 32.

8. Gerald and Caroline Greene, *S-M The Last Taboo* (New York: Grove Press, 1973).

9. See P. Brickman and Donald T. Campbell, "Hedonic Relativism and Planning the Good Society," in M. H. Appley (ed.), *Adaptation-level Theory: A Symposium* (New York: Academic Press, 1971); see also W. N. Dember and R. W. Earl, "Analysis of Exploratory, Manipulatory, and Curiosity Behavior," *Psychological Review,* LXIV (1957), 91-96; and Campbell, "On the Conflicts Between Biological and Social Evolution and Between Psychology and Moral Tradition," *American Psychologist,* December 1974, p. 1121.

10. Campbell, in *American Psychologist, loc. cit.*

11. Charles N. Cofer and Mortimer H. Appley, *Motivation: Theory and Research* (New York: Wiley, 1964), p. 682.

12. *Ibid.,* pp. 683f.

13. Calvin Hall and Gardner Lindzey, *Theories of Personality,* p. 476.

14. Carl R. Rogers, "Some New Challenges," *American Psychologist,* XXVIII (1973), 379-387.

15. Hans H. Strupp, "Clinical Psychology, Irrationalism, and the Erosion of Excellence," *American Psychologist,* XXXI (1976), 561-571.

16. Jacob Needleman, "Existential Psychoanalysis," in *The Encyclopedia of Philosophy* (New York: Macmillan, 1967), Vol. 3, p. 156. See also Jerome D. Frank, *Persuasion and Healing* (Baltimore: Johns Hopkins U. P., 1961; Schocken Paperback, 1963); William Schofield, *Psychotherapy: The Purchase of Friendship* (Englewood Cliffs, N.J.: Prentice-Hall, 1964); Thomas S. Szasz, *The Myth of Mental Illness* (New York: Harper and Brothers, 1961).

17. See for example, Frank, *op. cit.*

18. See Allen E. Bergin and Sol L. Garfield (eds.), *Handbook of*

Psychotherapy and Behavior Change: An Empirical Analysis (New York: Wiley, 1971).

19. Wayne Joosse, "Do Encounter Groups Work?" *The Reformed Journal*, XXIV, 2 (Feb. 1974), 8.

20. Hall and Lindzey, *op. cit.*, p. 326.

21. Carl R. Rogers, "A Theory of Therapy, Personality, and Interpersonal Relationships, As Developed in the Client-Centered Framework," in S. Koch (ed.), *Psychology: A Study of a Science*, p. 216; see also pp. 209, 213. Italics in original.

22. Ernest Becker, *Escape from Evil* (New York: Free Press, 1975), p. 137. This book and the same author's *Denial of Death* (New York: Free Press, 1973) provide a profound modern case for the tragic inevitability of evil, and thus a powerful rebuttal of denials of that evil by Fromm and other selfist thinkers.

23. Edward O. Wilson, "Competition and Aggressive Behavior," in J. F. Eisenberg & W. S. Dillon (eds.), *Man and Beast: Comparative Social Behavior* (Washington, D.C.: Smithsonian Institution Press, 1971). For an extensive bibliography see Donald T. Campbell, in *American Psychologist, loc. cit.*

24. Edward O. Wilson, *Sociobiology, the New Synthesis* (Cambridge, Mass.: Harvard U. P., 1975); quoted in *APA Monitor*, VI (Dec. 1975), 4.

25. Campbell, *op. cit.*, pp. 1120-21; see also the summary of Campbell's address in the *APA Monitor*, VI (Dec. 1975), 4-5. For responses to Campbell's address, see *The American Psychologist*, XXXI (May 1976), 341-384.

Chapter Four

1. Richard I. Evans, *Carl Rogers – The Man and His Ideas* (New York: Dutton, 1975), p. lxxxv.

2. Rogers and Stevens, *Person to Person*, p. 9.

3. Alasdair MacIntyre, "Existentialism," in *The Encyclopedia of Philosophy*, Vol. 3, p. 153.

4. *Ibid.*

Chapter Five

1. Erik H. Erikson, *Young Man Luther* (New York: Norton, 1958).

2. C. FitzSimons Allison, *Guilt, Anger and God* (New York: Seabury, 1972), p. 155.

3. *Ibid.*, p. 156.

4. *Ibid.*

5. Carl R. Rogers, *Becoming Partners: Marriage and Its Alternatives* (New York: Delacorte, 1972).

6. *Ibid.*, p. 8.

7. *Ibid.*, p. 212. Rogers' view of social experimentation as an aid to progress is an example of his debt to John Dewey, particularly *The Public and Its Problems* (New York: Holt, 1927).

8. See discussion of Edward Goldsmith's position in *Science*, CXCI (1976), 270-72; see also Paul R. Ehrlich, *The Population Bomb* (New York: Ballantine, 1968) and *The End of Affluence* (New York: Ballantine, 1974); Barry Commoner, *The Closing Circle* (New York: Knopf, 1971); and Meadows, Meadows, Randers, and Behrens, *The Limits to Growth* (New York: New American Library, 1972).

9. E. F. Schumacher, *Small is Beautiful* (New York: Harper & Row, 1973); see also *Science*, July 18, 1975, pp. 199-201; and Nicholas Georgescu-Roegen, *The Entropy Law and Economic Processes* (Cambridge, Mass.: Harvard U. P., 1971).

10. *New York Times*, Oct. 28, 1975, p. 68.

11. Robert L. Heilbroner, *An Inquiry Into the Human Prospect* (New York: Norton, 1974), pp. 25f.

Chapter Six

1. Frederick Engels, *Ludwig Feuerbach and the Outcome of Classical German Philosophy* (New York: International Publishers, 1941), p. 18. Quoted in E. G. Waring and F. W. Strothman (eds.), Ludwig Feuerbach, *The Essence of Christianity* (New York: Ungar Publishing Co., 1957), p. iii.

2. Feuerbach, *op. cit.*, pp. 26, 15, 11, 65.

3. Quoted in Feuerbach, *op. cit.*, p. vii; from Karl Marx, "Theses on Feuerbach," in Engels, *op. cit.*, p. 83.

4. *Ibid.*, p. 47.

5. Hayden V. White, "Ludwig Andreas Feuerbach," in *The Encyclopedia of Philosophy*, Vol. 3, p. 181.

6. See James H. Leuba, *A Psychological Study of Religion* (New York: Macmillan, 1912), Chapter XIII.

7. *Christianity and Progress* (New York: Association Press, 1922), p. 8.

8. Harry Emerson Fosdick, *As I See Religion* (New York: Harper, 1932), Chapter 2.

9. *On Being a Real Person* (New York: Harper, 1943), Chapter 2.

10. See discussion of Rogers in Hall and Lindzey, *Theories of Personality*, Chapter XII, and Rogers' article in Koch (ed.), *Psychology: A Study of a Science*.

11. Ellenberger, *The Discovery of the Unconscious* (New York: Basic Books, 1970), p. 595. Kurt Goldstein, whose organismic psychology emphasizes growth and integration, is another possible influence since he was in New York City from 1935 to about 1941. Fosdick does not cite Goldstein; and since Goldstein's major relevant work, *The Organism*, was not available in English till 1939, his influence on Fosdick probably is not significant.

12. Norman Vincent Peale, *The Art of Living* (New York: Abingdon-Cokesbury, 1937), p. 10.

13. For example, *Faith is the Answer* (New York: Abingdon-Cokesbury Press, n.d.).

14. Thomas C. Oden, *The Intensive Group Experience – The New Pietism* (Philadelphia: Westminster, 1972).

15. *Ibid.,* pp. 70f.

16. *Ibid.,* pp. 103-105.

17. Robert N. Sollod, "The Origins of Client-Centered Therapy," *Professional Psychology,* in press. Quotations are taken from the prepublication draft. Much of this section is based on this paper. Sollod also documents the origin of the client-centered or non-directive technique in the work of Goodwin Watson *et al.,* e.g., *American Journal of Orthopsychiatry,* XX (Oct. 1940), 698-709; and in the works of Otto Rank and Jessie Taft.

18. Rogers, *On Becoming a Person,* p. 8.

19. *Ibid.,* p. 9.

20. Sollod, *op. cit.,* p. 9.

21. William H. Kilpatrick, *Foundation of Method* (New York: Macmillan, 1926), pp. 191, 192, 198.

22. Sollod, *op. cit.,* p. 12, quoted from Kilpatrick, *How We Learn* (Calcutta: Association Press, 1929), p. 50.

23. See Carl Rogers, *Freedom to Learn* (Columbus: Merrill, 1969).

24. Carl Rogers, *Client-Centered Therapy* (Boston: Houghton-Mifflin, 1951), p. 386.

25. Carl Rogers in Koch (ed.), *Psychology: A Study of a Science,* Vol. 3, p. 209.

26. *Ibid.,* pp. 209, 216.

27. Christopher Lasch, "Sacrificing Freud," *New York Times Magazine,* Feb. 22, 1976, p. 11. See also Sollod, *op. cit.*

28. *Ibid.*

29. *Ibid.,* p. 72.

30. Freud quotations are from Paul Roazen, *Freud and His Followers* (New York: Knopf, 1975), p. 204; Sigmund Freud, *The Future of an Illusion,* trans. by W. D. Robson-Scott (Garden City, N.Y.: Doubleday Anchor, n.d.), p. 92.

Chapter Seven

1. O. H. Mowrer quotes the following "Psychiatric Folksong" by Anna Russell: "At three I had a feeling of/Ambivalence toward my brothers,/And so it follows naturally/I poisoned all my lovers./But now I'm happy; I have learned/The lesson this has taught;/That everything I do that's wrong/Is someone else's fault." "Sin, the Lesser of Two Evils," *American Psychologist,* XV (1960), 301-304.

2. Thomas A. Harris, *I'm OK — You're OK* (New York: Harper & Row, 1967), pp. 48f. Italics in original.

3. *Ibid.,* p. 51.

4. *Ibid.,* p. 52.

5. See, for example, Salvador Minuchin, *Families and Family Therapy* (Cambridge, Mass.: Harvard U. P., 1974).

Chapter Eight

1. Paul Ramsey, *Basic Christian Ethics* (New York: Scribners, 1950), p. 284.

2. Aleksandr I. Solzhenitsyn, *The Gulag Archipelago*, III-IV (New York: Harper & Row, 1975), pp. 615-16. See also Leonard Schapiro, "Disturbing, Fanatical, and Heroic," *New York Review of Books*, Nov. 13, 1975, p. 10; and Solzhenitsyn and others, *From Under the Rubble* (Boston: Little, Brown, 1975), esp. the essay by A.B.

3. O. Hobart Mowrer, "Sin, the Lesser of Two Evils," *American Psychologist*, XV (1960), 301-304.

4. *Ibid.*

5. Otto Baab, *The Theology of the Old Testament* (New York: Abingdon-Cokesbury, 1949), pp. 105, 110; quoted by Ramsey, *op. cit.*, p. 298.

6. See Paul Zweig, *The Heresy of Self-Love* (New York: Harper & Row, 1968).

7. On Pelagius, see Robert F. Evans, *Pelagius: Inquiries and Reappraisals* (New York: Seabury, 1968).

8. Erich Fromm, *Psychoanalysis and Religion*, p. 34.

9. Erich Fromm, *The Art of Loving* (New York: Harper, 1956), p. 63.

10. Quoted by Otto Karrar (ed.), *Meister Eckhart Speaks* (London: Blackfriars, 1957), p. 41. See also J. M. Clark, *The Great German Mystics* (Oxford, 1949) and Etienne Gilson, *Christian Philosophy in the Middle Ages* (New York: Random House, 1955).

11. See for example Abraham H. Maslow, *Religions, Values, and Peak Experiences* (New York: Viking, 1970). Some of Maslow's later writings go beyond humanistic selfism into what is now called transpersonal psychology. This vertical emphasis derives from his hierarchical theory of personality which clearly implies a series of higher and higher levels of mental life.

12. Saint Bernard, *On the Love of God* (*De Diligendo Deo*), tr. Sister Penelope (London: Mowbrays, 1950), ch. 9.

13. *Ibid.*, p. 64.

14. *Ibid.*, pp. 66f. See Etienne Gilson, *The Mystical Theory of St. Bernard* (New York: Sheed and Ward, 1940), for a fine discussion of St. Bernard's major contribution to spiritual psychology.

15. Martin Luther, "Treatise on Christian Liberty," in *Works* (Philadelphia-Muhlenberg Press, 1943), II, 342; quoted by Ramsey, *op. cit.*, p. 101.

16. Chapter xiv; quoted from *A Diary of Readings*, compiled by John Baillie (New York: Scribners, 1955), Day 140.

17. Fromm, *Art of Loving*, p. 60.

18. See Heinz Kohut, *The Analysis of the Self: A Systematic Approach to the Psychoanalytic Treatment of Narcissistic Personality Disorders* (New York: International Univ. Press, 1971); and Otto Kernberg, *Borderline Conditions and Psychological Narcissism* (New York: Jason Aronson, 1975).

19. C. S. Lewis, "Christianity and Literature," in *Christian Reflections* (ed. Walter Hooper) (Grand Rapids: Eerdmans, 1967), pp. 6f.

20. *Ibid.*, p. 7.

Chapter Nine

1. D. O. Hebb, "What psychology is about," *American Psychologist,* XXIX (1974), 71-79.

2. Irving Kristol, "Thoughts on Reading About a Number of Summer-Camp Cabins Covered with Garbage," *The New York Times Magazine,* Nov. 17, 1974, p. 38.

3. Malachi B. Martin, "Death at Sunset," *National Review,* Nov. 22, 1974, p. 1356.

4. Ernest Becker, *The Denial of Death,* p. 164.

5. Further information about persecution is available in such sources as Solzhenitsyn, *et al., From Under the Rubble;* and the journal *Religion in Communist Lands,* published by The Centre for the Study of Religion and Communism, Keston College, Heathfield Road, Keston Kent, England BR2 6BA.

Chapter Ten

1. This section is influenced by a number of sources, particularly Walter Wink, *The Bible in Human Transformation* (Philadelphia: Fortress, 1973), though his analysis of the final stage is incompatible with mine; also Evelyn B. Vitz, "Inside/Outside: Guillaume de Lorris' *Roman de la Rose,*" *Yale French Studies,* in press 1977, particularly on the medieval view of the self.

2. See Hans H. Strupp, "Clinical Psychology, Irrationalism, and the Erosion of Excellence," *American Psychologist,* XXI (1976), 561-571; and Paul Meehl, *Psychodiagnosis* (Minneapolis: Univ. of Minnesota Press, 1973).

3. Walter Wink, *op. cit.,* pp. 25f.

4. Hans Jonas, *The Phenomenon of Life* (New York: Harper & Row, 1966), pp. 195f.; quoted by Wink, *op. cit.,* pp. 39f.

5. *Ibid.,* p. 196.

6. Herbert Hendin, *The Age of Sensation* (New York: Norton, 1975), p. 6.

7. *Ibid.,* p. 13.

8. *Ibid.,* p. 125.

9. *Ibid.,* pp. 60-61, 72.

10. *Ibid.,* p. 259.

11. Andy Warhol, *The Philosophy of Andy Warhol (From A to B and Back Again)* (New York: Harcourt Brace Jovanovich, 1975), p. 51.

12. Hendin, *op. cit.,* p. 296.

13. *Ibid.,* p. 332.

14. *Ibid.,* pp. 257, 256.

15. *Ibid.,* p. 336.

16. Paul Ricoeur, *Symbolism of Evil* (New York: Harper & Row, 1967), p. 351.

Chapter Eleven

1. Ernest Becker, *The Denial of Death*, p. 268.
2. Abraham H. Maslow, *Religions, Values, and Peak Experiences.*
3. Ernest Becker, *Escape from Evil*, p. 164.

Index of Subjects

Index of Personal Names